2008

AMERICA'S ROLE IN

ASIA

ASIAN AND AMERICAN VIEWS

Recommendations for U.S. policy from both sides of the Pacific

The Asia Foundation

AMERICA'S ROLE IN ASIA: ASIAN AND AMERICAN VIEWS

First Edition
Copyright 2008 by The Asia Foundation
All rights reserved. No part of this book may be reproduced
without written permission by The Asia Foundation.

The Asia Foundation gratefully acknowledges AIG and Chevron
Corporation for their generous support of the America's Role in
Asia project.

The Asia Foundation

465 California Street 9th Floor, San Francisco CA 94104
ISBN 1-892325-08-X

Printed in U.S.A.

TABLE OF CONTENTS

FOREWORD

For more than half a century, a major objective of The Asia Foundation has been to foster greater understanding and dialogue between the United States and Asia in order to advance our mission of promoting a peaceful, prosperous, just, and open Asia-Pacific region. We believe that if workable solutions to common problems are to be found, perspectives from both sides of the Pacific must be heard. The Foundation's extensive relationships and comprehensive development programs provide extraordinary access to a wide range of U.S. and Asian leaders, both inside and outside of government, who can provide those perspectives.

This year, the Foundation has organized and supported the fourth in a series of quadrennial reports on *America's Role in Asia*, which seek to examine critical bilateral and transnational issues through workshops and discussions on both sides of the Pacific. These discussions have culminated in the following papers, written by American and Asian scholars, which provide policymakers and business leaders with concrete recommendations on how to address challenges and opportunities in Asia – from stability on the Korean peninsula, conflict in Afghanistan, and the global war on terror; to energy security, environmental degradation, and Asia's regional architecture, trade, and investment.

The project's American task force was chaired by two of America's most distinguished former diplomats, Ambassador Michael Armacost, Shorenstein Senior Fellow at the Asia Pacific Center at Stanford University, and Ambassador J. Stapleton Roy, Vice Chairman of Kissinger International Associates. The American task force produced 15 essays that are both specific to bilateral relationships and regional in scope, and address a range of issues that the new U.S. administration will inherit in January.

In Asia, three groups of senior policy specialists led by Ambassador Han Sung-Joo, Chairman of the Asan Institute in Seoul; Ambassador Tommy Koh, Chairman of Singapore's Institute of Policy Studies; and Dr. C. Raja Mohan, Professor at the Rajanathan School of International Studies in Singapore, came together in Seoul, Singapore, and New Delhi to provide their informed Asian perspectives on U.S. policies and roles in Northeast, Southeast, and South Asia.

Comparisons between the two reports are both useful and inevitable. Nevertheless, we believe that each report should stand on its own, articulating aspects of the complex and multiple dimensions of a relationship that is vital to the security and economic prosperity of Americans and Asians alike.

The Asia Foundation is grateful to the five chairs for their consideration, cooperation, and commitment toward the *America's Role in Asia* project throughout 2008, and to all the other participants in the project. We also would like to thank the American International Group (AIG) and Chevron Corporation for their generous financial support. Finally, this project could not have been launched, much less successfully concluded, without the support of many Asia Foundation staff in 17 offices across Asia, as well as our offices in San Francisco and Washington, D.C.; particularly Hope Stewart, Katherine Brown, George Varughese, Nancy Kelly, Amy Ovalle, Kye Young, Gordon Hein, Allen Choate, Nancy Yuan, Rajendra Abhyankar, T.D. Aggrawal, Chun-Sung Moon, Soyeon Jun, Edward Reed, and Scott Snyder.

Doug Bereuter
President, The Asia Foundation

John J. Brandon
Director, International Relations Programs
The Asia Foundation

ASIAN VIEWS OF AMERICA'S ROLE IN ASIA 2008: AN OVERVIEW

Han Sung-Joo
Tommy Koh
C. Raja Mohan

Introduction

The election of a new American president is an event of great importance not only to the United States, but to the entire world. Asians from all walks of life have been following the 2008 presidential primaries with great interest and admiration. The world has seen a democratic process where neither wealth nor pedigree — race nor gender — are obstacles to securing America's highest office. Asians are looking at the November 2008 election with great anticipation and are curious about the next American president's foreign policy toward a multi-polar world where countries like China, India, and Russia are increasing their power and influence.

America's 44th president will face many challenges once in office. How to rebuild trust in America after its unpopular invasion of Iraq? How to revive the American economy without resorting to protectionist measures in a global trading system? How to defeat terrorism without creating the impression that Islam is the enemy? How to interface with the international community in utilizing multilateral institutions to uphold international law and foster justice in the world?

How America responds to these and other challenges will determine its future relations with all three sub-regions of the Asia-Pacific: Northeast Asia, Southeast Asia, and South Asia.

As the world's preeminent power, the U.S.'s influence is felt throughout the globe. Asia is no exception. From Japan to Afghanistan, the United States plays a crucial role in the security, political, and economic affairs of the region. The United States is either the first or second largest trading partner of almost every Asian nation in all three sub-regions. Although U.S. trade with Asia is expanding — as a percentage of market share, it is declining. Intra-Asian trade now constitutes 55 percent of the region's trade with the world. In this decade, China has replaced the United States as the number one trading partner of Japan, South Korea, Taiwan, and a number of Southeast Asian countries. Trends indicate that China will be South Asia's largest trading partner in the near future. But Asians remain concerned that the anti-free trade rhetoric espoused during the American presidential primaries will impede any possibility of successfully completing multilateral trade negotiations under the Doha Development Agenda (DDA) in the World Trade Organization (WTO).

As the world's preeminent power, the U.S.'s influence is felt throughout the globe. Asia is no exception. From Japan to Afghanistan, the United States plays a crucial role in the security, political, and economic affairs of the region.

Although the United States has been "the" regional power in Asia since the end of World War II, there is now some uncertainty about the relevance of U.S. power given current regional dynamics. The United States may still hold the balance of power in Asia, but does this mean that the U.S. necessarily holds the most influence? Gradually emerging is a multilateral Asian architecture based on a series of increasingly shared norms around interstate relations and security. In recent years, Asians have been discussing the idea of "East Asian community building." Although the growth of such multilateralism had a late start compared with Europe, the past two decades have seen progress with the establishment of the Asia Pacific Economic Cooperation (APEC) Forum, the ASEAN Regional Forum (ARF), ASEAN Plus Three (China, Japan, and South Korea) — and now, the East Asia Summit (EAS). The United States is a member of the first two groupings, but not the latter two.

Creating an East Asian Community is a long-term endeavor. A community including China, Japan, India, and Australia — along with the nations of ASEAN, South Korea, and New Zealand — is so vast and heterogeneous that its movement is bound to be slow and incremental. There are two legs to an East Asian Community: economic and political. The economic leg is becoming increasingly stronger with significant trade and investment flows between and among the Asian nations. In contrast, however, the political leg is relatively underdeveloped. The remarkable differences among Asian countries in history, culture, religious traditions, and levels of economic development contribute to American skepticism that creating an East Asian Community is not possible. But the U.S. needs to understand that the growth of an East Asian Community stems from a natural desire in the region to forge ties and create a coherent regional identity. There is a growing sense of Asian regionalism. If the U.S. continues to take a narrow perspective on this issue, it stands to lose influence in the region.

Even if the United States was firmly committed to an East Asian Community and wanted full membership, Asian countries may or may not welcome U.S. participation. Many Asians have been surprised by the U.S.'s passive attitude toward the East Asia Summit (EAS), and suspect it is due to American preoccupation with the wars in Iraq and Afghanistan and other problems in the Middle East. Nonetheless, even if the United States never joins the EAS, Asian nations must still engage with the U.S. as a dialogue partner. Any discussion on how to solve the global challenges we face — from energy security, environmental degradation, and transnational crime; to the global war on terror; to trade, investment, and finance — must include the United States. Asia wants the U.S. to be an effective, global leader at a time when China, India, and Russia are increasing their own regional and global power and influence.

The U.S. needs to understand that the growth of an East Asian Community stems from a natural desire in the region to forge ties and create a coherent regional identity... If the U.S. continues to take a narrow perspective on this issue, it stands to lose influence in the region.

For Asians, traditional security and economic issues remain important foundations for U.S. engagement in the region, but energy security, the environment, natural disaster response, and other issues are becoming increasingly salient.

With the price of oil skyrocketing to $140 per barrel, the Asia-Pacific region needs a cohesive energy security policy. The United States is the world's largest consumer of energy — while China, Japan, India, and South Korea are, respectively, the second, third, sixth, and seventh largest consumers in the world. Eighty percent of the world's oil and liquefied natural gas (LNG) either passes through – or comes from – Southeast Asia, increasing the region's geo-strategic importance as a conduit, consumer, and supplier of energy. By 2015, 75 percent of all oil from the Persian Gulf will be exported to Asian markets. Any successful energy policy must be a collective effort among Asian countries in all three sub-regions together with the United States.

The United States and Asia also have a critical role to play in the environmental sustainability of our planet. The Asia-Pacific region accounts for 60 percent of the world's population and 50 percent of global economic output. The United States and China are the world's largest emitters of greenhouse gases. Environmental degradation throughout Asia is severe. Global warming and economic expansion have caused significant air and water pollution and scarcity levels from Seoul to Kabul. Tropical rainforests are being depleted and rare species of flora and fauna are becoming extinct. Asian governments are concerned that if they become more ecologically responsible, it will incur a high cost on their states' economic growth. The U.S.'s 2001 refusal to sign the Kyoto Protocol without providing an alternative was a missed opportunity for the United States to provide leadership on how to protect our planet. The U.S. could restore its leadership in environmental policy should it decide to work with multilateral fora (ASEAN, South Asian Association for Regional Cooperation, APEC, ARF) to develop ways to curb greenhouse gas emissions; and to share technology to promote energy efficiency, clean and renewable energy, carbon capture and sequestration, and other relevant technologies.

Over the past four years, the Asia-Pacific region has endured natural disasters that have brought death and destruction on significant scales. These include the 2004 tsunami in Indonesia, Sri Lanka, Thailand, and India; the 2008 Nargis cyclone in Myanmar (formerly known as Burma); and devastating earthquakes in Pakistan and China in 2006 and 2008, respectively. The United States recently proposed the idea of developing a standing coordinated mechanism to respond to these types of catastrophes. With U.S. leadership, it would be timely for the ASEAN Regional Forum (ARF) to embrace this proposal and we hope the next U.S. president will act on this initiative.

Promoting democracy and the protection of human rights has been a major thrust in U.S. policy. But while conducting the war on terrorism, the United States has been inconsistent with its own principles in dealing with terrorist suspects and political prisoners in Guantanamo and abroad. The U.S. has demanded international isolation of Myanmar for its harsh military rule while seeking engagement and dialogue with the dictatorial regime in North Korea. The United States would be well advised to set a good example of upholding the very values it espouses. U.S. allies in the region are acutely aware of America's poor image among their own public and want the next administration's foreign policy to pay special attention to public diplomacy. How the U.S. engages not just Asian governments, but the Asian people through education and cultural opportunities should be of equal consideration to the above issues when strategizing and implementing foreign policy. Both Americans and Asians will benefit if the political, intellectual, and cultural bridges between our peoples are strengthened.

This overview captures only a handful of issues that resonated in all three Asian sub-regional meetings held in Seoul, Singapore, and New Delhi. Below are a set of recommendations that we, the project's three Asian Chairs, felt were the most important. But in addition to these issues and recommendations, the ensuing chapters of this report delve into greater detail about the U.S. foreign policy concerns most important to all three sub-regions — from security on the Korean peninsula and the Afghanistan-Pakistan border to U.S. relations with China, India, and ASEAN. We believe if the 44th president of the United States and the next Congress that assumes office in January 2009 adopts these recommendations, U.S. relations with our region as a whole will greatly improve.

Specifically, these recommendations include:

1. The U.S. should actively support a regional architecture in Asia. Bilateral relations are important, but greater emphasis should be placed on multinational diplomacy around political, economic, and security issues. This includes signing the Treaty of Amity and Cooperation (TAC), which, at a minimum, would allow the United States to be an effective dialogue partner with members of the East Asia Summit. The U.S. signature would also illustrate its confidence in regional organizations such as ASEAN, ARF, and APEC.

2. The new U.S. administration should take two critical steps toward improving trade with the region. First, seek an early and successful conclusion of the Doha Development Round (DDA) under the auspices of the World Trade Organization (WTO). Second, Congress should give the 44th president fast-track trade negotiating authority, through which it could ratify the U.S.-Korea Free Trade Agreement.

3. The next administration should work with Asian regional institutions to begin a dialogue on energy security and climate change — especially in the area of curbing greenhouse gas emis-

sions – and to bring the post-Kyoto negotiations to a successful conclusion. The United States must share with its Asian partners its expertise in energy efficiency, clean and renewable energy, carbon capture and sequestration, and other technologies.

4. Over the past several years, the United States, despite irritants, has been able to maintain sound and sensible relations with China. The 44th president should not be tempted to score domestic political points by using contentious rhetoric toward China. The new administration should take advantage of China's declared intention not to upset the status-quo and its willingness to maintain good relations with the United States.

5. A long-term military and development commitment to Afghanistan must be clearly and repeatedly articulated. There is a widespread assumption in Asia (particularly South Asia) that U.S. attention to Afghanistan is, at best, short-term. If the United States prepares to draw down its forces in Iraq in the coming years, it should be in a position to enhance U.S. troop presence in Afghanistan. Such a commitment must be supplemented by a range of economic and development measures that increase Afghanistan's national capacity to effectively govern and provide for its own security in all 34 provinces.

6. The United States should also help Pakistan and Afghanistan resolve their long-standing border issues in a diplomatic and nuanced way. The United States must undertake a significant effort to win political support among the Pashtun tribes, separate them from al-Qaeda and the Taliban, and make them stakeholders in the war against terror. The United States must help the Pakistani and Afghan governments strengthen the traditional Pashtun tribal structures.

7. The transformation of the relationship with India has been a major contribution of the Bush administration to the evolution of U.S. policy in Asia and has had strong support from the Democratic Party. Building on this bipartisan consensus, the next administration must complete the implementation of the historic civil nuclear initiative between the two countries and consolidate the strategic partnership with New Delhi.

8. As the non-proliferation of weapons of mass destruction (WMD) emerges at the top of the new administration's agenda, Washington will need a comprehensive strategy. In East Asia, the new U.S. president would be well advised to continue with the North Korea policy adopted by the Bush administration in spring 2007. More broadly, the United States can help reinvigorate the global nuclear order by agreeing to significant reductions in the American and Russian nuclear arsenals; encouraging China and India to contribute more to the maintenance of the non-proliferation regime; boosting the institutional capacity of the International Atomic Energy Agency (the principal watchdog working to prevent the spread of nuclear weapons); and balancing the competing imperatives of increased use of nuclear energy for electric power generation around the world.

9. Finally, the United States must devote more attention to its public diplomacy efforts with the Asian people. This includes strengthening educational, intellectual, and cultural ties to civil society organizations and Asian opinion leaders.

THE U.S. ROLE IN NORTHEAST ASIA

Han Sung-Joo

Overview: Changing Political Landscape

At the end of the first decade of the 21st century, the majority of Northeast Asian countries remain on reasonably good terms with the United States, maintaining for the most part peaceful, productive, and cooperative relations. The United States has managed to keep relations with China on an even keel. It is also reshaping and streamlining the alliances with Japan and South Korea in a way that strives to meet the needs of the emerging geopolitical realities of Northeast Asia and the demands of the U.S.'s own military structure and capabilities. Even with regard to North Korea, the United States is hopeful about resolving the nuclear weapons issues within the context of the Six-Party Talks. This is despite the fact that North Korea has previously been a thorn in U.S. foreign policy toward Northeast Asia. However, Northeast Asia is undergoing significant changes in its international relations. The next U.S. administration will be dealing with a regional situation that is quite different from what it has been over the years. Several developments characterize the changing geopolitical landscape in Northeast Asia.

First, there are leadership changes occurring in many countries of Northeast Asia. In China, a fifth generation of leaders is emerging in the aftermath of the 17th Party Congress, which took place in the fall of 2007. Even though President Hu Jintao continues to lead the country, he is now joined by younger leaders with professional backgrounds who subscribe to both a nationalistic and pragmatic outlook on policy. In Japan, a succession of leaders from Junichiro Koizumi to Shinjo Abe to Yasuo Fukuda has left the country still searching for an effective government that can undertake needed domestic reforms and conduct robust foreign relations. The recent elections in South Korea and Taiwan produced more pragmatic and conservative presidents. However, the new South Korean president, Lee Myung-bak, is experiencing serious political difficulties and a dramatic loss of popularity at the outset of his presidential term. Taiwan's Ma Ying-jeou promises to bring about more amicable and productive relations with the mainland under the policy of promoting cross-Strait peace and cooperation. Russia also elected a new president, after 10 years with Vladimir Putin in office — though many predict that Putin will likely continue to exercise power as the prime minister. Finally, the United States will elect a new president after eight years of George W. Bush's administration. Leadership change in most of the regional countries in Northeast Asia will have a significant effect on U.S. relations within the region.

Second, even as the traditional security and economic issues remain important, new sets of issues — including resource competition, environment and climate change, pandemic diseases and other natural disasters, humanitarian problems, proliferation of weapons of mass destruction, and domestic governance — are increasingly gaining salience in regional and international relations, as they will in America's relations with the region.

Third, with the strong growth of key countries such as China, Russia, and India in the last few years, we are witnessing the return of big power politics in the region. Their rise means the need for more consultation, closer cooperation and better coordination among them in order to achieve mutual benefits in political, security, and economic areas. The newly emerging big powers increasingly demand recognition of their regional and international presence, status, and weight — a fact which requires the development of a more multi-polar framework as well as multilateral processes and institutions.

Fourth, the return of big power politics is also likely to provoke a change in the pattern of regional politics. Even though bilateral alliances will remain an important element in Northeast Asian international relations, the region is also witnessing the emergence of a regional system of cooperation, which will supplement the competitive nature of alliances.

Even though bilateral alliances will remain an important element in Northeast Asian international relations, the region is also witnessing the emergence of a regional system of cooperation, which will supplement the competitive nature of alliances.

Fifth, changes are taking place in the way international affairs are conducted. Even as military power remains salient, soft power is gaining importance as more countries are becoming adept at cultivating and utilizing it. Although unilateral and bilateral arrangements remain important, multilateral consultations, arrangements, and institutions are becoming more salient and indispensable. International relations are increasingly becoming less of a zero-sum game.

Sixth, the relative importance of Asia as a whole, and Northeast Asia in particular, is growing vis-à-vis other regions in the world. The Asia-Pacific region is home to several of the world's largest economies (present and prospective) — including Japan, China, India, Russia, and the United States. It is in Northeast Asia where these economies intersect and where America's largest trading partners are located. Many scholars predict that this trend will continue and accelerate during the next few decades.

Seventh, the security paradigm in the region is shifting. In the past, the United States created alliances with Japan and South Korea in order to contain Soviet expansion, prevent another outbreak of war in the Korean Peninsula, defend Japan, and maintain a leadership position in the Asian Continent. Today, these alliances are deemed necessary to maintain balance vis-à-vis emerging powers such as China and Russia; for peace and security in the Asian region; to keep sea lanes of communication (SLOCs) open; to prevent proliferation and transport of weapons of mass destruction and the means of their delivery; to fight a global war on terrorism; and to maintain U.S. military presence in the region for the above purposes.

Eighth, we are witnessing the globalization of regional affairs and the strengthening of links between the East Asia region and the rest of the world. What happens in the Middle East, for example, has relevance and impact on East Asia. Middle East security issues not only affect security and terrorism in Asia, but also the amount of attention the United States can and will devote to Asia. It will also have a direct bearing on Asia's energy security and supply.

Ninth, also part of the changing landscape is Mongolia, undergoing leadership change after July's parliamentary elections. Whereas Northeast Asia is one of the most economically developed regions in the world, Mongolia is a poor nation with many significant economic and social development needs. Mongolia should be given much credit for its efforts over the past two decades in developing into a democratic society; and it wants to be more politically, economically, and socially integrated into a region surrounded by giant powers (China and Japan) and some of the world's most economically developed societies (Japan and South Korea).

Finally, East Asian countries are experiencing a phenomenon that can be called a "democratization of foreign policy," as citizens and the civil society become more interested and engaged in foreign affairs...The effect is greater involvement of the non-governmental sector in foreign affairs and the imposition of greater constraints on the government in conducting foreign policy.

Finally, East Asian countries are experiencing a phenomenon that can be called a "democratization of foreign policy," as citizens and the civil society become more interested and engaged in foreign affairs. As the economies of East Asian countries become more globalized, people feel the effects of foreign relations more directly and keenly on their daily lives. At the same time, as different means of communication become more readily available and extensive, public consciousness spreads in conjunction with the expanding horizon of information. The effect is greater involvement of the non-governmental sector in foreign affairs and the imposition of greater constraints on the government in conducting foreign policy.

1. U.S.-China Relations

As China focuses on maintaining high economic growth, its leaders recognize that it is in its best interest to maintain a good relationship with the United States. China continues to value highly its economic and political relationship with the United States. Despite a brief crisis that arose during the early phase of the Bush administration (the downing of the U.S.'s EP-3 surveillance plane), China and the United States have worked on building better relations. The exchange of visits by top leaders in the two countries contributes to and demonstrates the willingness to resolve even some of the most troublesome issues in an amicable manner.

However, one can still envision friction emerging between the United States, a status-quo power, and China, a revisionist power, over such issues as Taiwan, human rights, and trade. Even as cross-Strait relations show prospects of improvement due to mutual accommodation and increased exchange (of personnel and goods), China is concerned about the U.S. weapons sales policy toward Taiwan. The United States is also wary of China's trade policy and human rights records.

Transitions between U.S. administrations have historically exacerbated existing problems in the U.S.-China bilateral relationship for temporary periods of time. In the past, each administration discovered over time that advancing U.S. interests through cooperation with Beijing was a more effective strategy than pursuing contentious relations. There are concerns about whether this pattern of peace and cooperation can continue as the United States increasingly worries about China's growing economic and military power and its burgeoning political influence. A new administration must draw from past experience in order to put the U.S.-China bilateral relationship on sound footing from the beginning. The next U.S. administration should prioritize its dealings with Beijing on issues such as Korea, Taiwan, trade and financial differences, and regional cooperation.

A new administration must draw from past experience in order to put the U.S.-China bilateral relationship on sound footing from the beginning. The next U.S. administration should prioritize its dealings with Beijing on issues such as Korea, Taiwan, trade and financial differences, and regional cooperation.

China suspects that the United States is trying to counter-balance, if not contain, it through alliances with Japan, Australia, and South Korea and by befriending India. China also has misgivings about the missile defense system that the United States is promoting — and that Japan and Australia are joining — as being directed against China. The United States is concerned about China's growing economic and military power and burgeoning political influence; wary of the possibility of the emergence of China as a possible competitor or challenger to its interests; and is worried about the possibility of China using force vis-à-vis Taiwan. The United

States also has misgivings over China's policies regarding human rights and minority groups; while China complains about the United States meddling in what it considers its domestic affairs.

However, China and the United States seem to be recognizing the reality of interdependence and the necessity of maintaining good relations with each other. They are learning to manage a series of tough issues such as the Taiwan Strait, the Korean Peninsula, and economic co-dependency. Investment and trade are on the rise. They have collaborated closely on the North Korean nuclear issue. China has not sought to upset the status quo, nor does it wish to jeopardize relations with the United States. The United States has been encouraging China to become a "responsible stakeholder" in both the region and the world. The two countries are trying to convince each other, and the world, that they are not a threat to each other.

2. Economic Relations with China

Over the years, China not only posted a high rate of economic growth (more than 9.5 percent growth for the past 26 years); but also acted as the locomotive in the East Asian growth as a whole, which grew by 8.7 percent in 2007 and is expected to attain a growth rate of 8.2 percent in 2008. According to some experts, the robust growth of China and the resultant growth in trade with China helped both the United States and Japan post positive growth for the years 2006 and 2007. Both China and the United States recognize the importance of their interdependent economic relationship. The bilateral economic relationship was a priority topic when President Bush met Chinese President Hu Jintao in Washington in April, 2006. The two countries subsequently launched the U.S.-China Strategic Economic Dialogue (SED) which has become an important driver for the trade relations of the two countries. In the past couple of years, the United States and China have reached agreements on food safety, the environment, energy, and investment. China is interested in continued access to the U.S. market, technology, and universities. The United States wants to help complete the transition of China to a market-based, open economy which will contribute to the stability and prosperity of the world.

At the same time, China's rapid economic growth presents certain problems for the United States and the rest of the region. One is the strain on key commodities such as energy and food, driving their prices higher and causing competition to secure those resources. Second, at least for the United States, the trade deficit continues to mount — partly as a result of other Asian economies relying on China for the substantial processing and final assembly of products, which results in circuitous trade via China; and also partly because of the increasingly strong U.S. demand for Chinese goods.

While continuing to promote the mutual opening of markets with China, the next U.S. administration will have to make efforts to persuade the U.S. public and Congress that there are mutual benefits of liberalization measures for trade, finance, and investment.

The trade deficit and the growing number of job exports to China are creating a backlash in the United States, with some experts and commentators arguing that increasing investment in China and expanding trade only contribute to the growing exportation of jobs and loss of work in the United States. As a result, free trade agreements (FTAs) and other trade liberalization measures such as the Doha Development Agenda (DDA) have become unpopular topics in U.S. domestic politics. While continuing to promote the mutual opening of markets with China, the next U.S. administration will have to make efforts to persuade the U.S. public and Congress that there are mutual benefits of liberalization measures for trade, finance, and investment.

3. U.S.-Japan Relations

The new post-Cold War generation of leaders that is emerging in Japan is trying to find ways to reinvigorate the Japanese economy, regain the "ordinary state" status that they feel it lost after the Second World War, and cope with the challenge of China's growing influence and power in the region. Japan hopes to produce an effective government to carry out those tasks. Japan is concerned that the United States does not fully appreciate the frustrations that the Japanese feel as they seek to determine what strategy can best address these challenges. Moreover, coordination in successive U.S. administrations of the political, economic, and security aspects of the U.S.-Japan relationship have been less than optimal. A new U.S. administration should take action that would put this vital relationship on more sound footing in the next decade and beyond.

Like some other key countries such as the United States and South Korea, Japan finds itself heavily dependent on business with China for its economic recovery and solvency. Japan is trying to boost its security and cope with China's challenge through increased defense spending and maintaining a staunch alliance with the United States. However, even as the United States recognizes Japan as its most important ally in Asia, it often gives the impression that Japan's cooperation is taken for granted.

On the North Korean nuclear issue in particular, Japan, which used to be on the side of the United States before the latter's change of stance, has now become the odd man out in the six-party process with its preoccupation with the North Korean abduction of Japanese citizens, an issue that has not been resolved to Japan's satisfaction. Even though Kim Jong-Il admitted the abduction to the visiting then-Japanese Prime Minister Koizumi, North Korea failed to completely account for the fate of all of the Japanese citizens abducted. To Japan, the United States appeared to proceed without due consideration of the position and interest of Japan. It was inevitable that Japan felt left out. Ultimately, however, a formula will be found to address Japan's concerns related to the issue and Japan will feel it is in its own interest to join the six-party process as a full-fledged participant. Although Japan will continue to have misgivings about a deal with North Korea without a satisfactory resolution of the abduction issue, it will choose to join the other five members of the Six-Party Talks as they seek to declare success with what is at best an incomplete deal in denuclearizing North Korea.

4. U.S.-ROK Relations

The 21st century began with strains in U.S.-Korea relations, particularly over how to deal with North Korea and the nuclear issue — the United States took the hard-line and South Korea was more accommodating. There was a rise in manifestations of anti-

American sentiments in Korea, which disappointed many Americans who thought Koreans were being "ungrateful" for the U.S. support during the Korean War, and its overall democratic and economic development. In due course, however, the relationship improved and recovered its solvency. South Korea sent troops to Iraq, which became the third-largest contingent after the United States and the United Kingdom. The two governments agreed on the relocation of the U.S. troops in Korea and South Korea accepted the principle of strategic flexibility of U.S. troops in Korea. They also agreed on the transfer of the war-time operational control of the Korean armed forces by the year 2012. Once the United States agreed to the six-party agreement in the spring of 2007, the U.S. and South Korea even agreed on how to deal with the North Korean nuclear issue. The two countries also successfully negotiated, concluded, and signed a free trade agreement; pending only the approval of the U.S. Congress and the National Assembly of the Republic of Korea.

However, as the large-scale protests in Korea over the beef import agreement with the United States demonstrated, there is still widespread, latent anti-American sentiment in South Korea that can be mobilized to action given an opportune issue and momentum. This is despite the fact that, according to a March 2008 Pew Research survey, an overwhelming majority of Koreans (70 percent) hold favorable views toward the United States — a higher percentage that can be found than in any other country among the 24 major countries surveyed.

Furthermore, South Korea is understandably concerned about the possibility of getting involved in a conflict between the United States and China. Hence, South Korea is hesitant to join the missile defense project of the United States, a project in which Japan is actively involved. In a similar vein, South Korea takes a lukewarm attitude toward the Proliferation Security Initiative (PSI) of the United States, a project intended to interdict transportation of weapons of mass destruction and their related material and equipment. It is for this reason that United States Secretary of State Condoleezza Rice publicly refers to South Korea as a "partner" while Japan and Australia are considered as "allies."

Despite the end of the Cold War, the ROK-U.S. alliance is still useful and valuable to both countries. The ROK-U.S. alliance has gone beyond the original objective of defending Korea against North Korea's military threat, containing the Soviet Union, and defending Japan; and has evolved into a partnership contributing to peace and stability not only in East Asia but also throughout the world. While deterring war, the alliance will be useful in inducing strategic change in North Korea so that it will cooperate toward stability and peace on the Korean peninsula.

The ROK-U.S. alliance seems ready to transcend beyond its focus on traditional security threats. With a view to pursuing universal values such as freedom, human rights, democracy, and a market economy, the alliance can mature into a cooperative partnership not only for the Korean Peninsula, but also for the Asia-Pacific region and the world as a whole. The next U.S. president will have a good opportunity to pursue these goals as South Korea's president, Lee Myung-bak, is eager to strengthen its alliance with the United States and establish a comprehensive relationship in all areas ranging from security and economy to culture and values.

5. North Korea and Nuclear Proliferation

On the proliferation front, after several years of wrangling over North Korean nuclear weapons, cautious optimism is beginning to emerge. The North Korean nuclear negotiation appears to be making progress with the prospect that the Six-Party Talks will seal a deal that will stop the North Korean nuclear weapons program.

What is the basis for this optimism? The answer is that the Bush administration, after initially denouncing the Clinton administration's handling of the North Korean nuclear issue as reflected in the 1994 Geneva Agreed Framework, finally came around to actually emulating the former policy. Until February 2007, the Bush administration kept a hard line on North Korea and the nuclear issue in particular. The United States was against bilateral talks with a member of "the axis of evil" and against "rewarding" North Korea for its bad behavior. Since the spring of 2007, however, the Bush administration began formulating a new policy of negotiating with North Korea on a bilateral basis. It would reward North Korea for its "good behavior," that is, for freezing, declaring, and "disabling" its nuclear weapons program. Even without a complete dismantlement of the nuclear program or a full declaration of nuclear and transfer activities, the Bush administration is willing to provide rewards in the form of lifting North Korea from the list of countries supporting terrorism, removing restrictions on North Korean trade under the Trading with the Enemy Act, providing energy (heavy oil) together with other countries and food (500,000 tons of corn and wheat), and giving security assurances.

North Korea must have felt vindicated when its bomb testing in October 2006 prompted the United States to change its attitude toward North Korea — accepting it as a negotiating partner and moving the goal post in such a way that it became easier for North Korea to score. Now North Korea has both the need and opportunity to coax the United States into a deal, imperfect though it may be. North Korea badly needs to have U.S. economic sanctions lifted. It desperately needs to get assistance in energy and food at a time when the prices of both commodities are soaring high and both China and South Korea are becoming less generous with assistance to North Korea. Pyongyang now has the opportunity to make a deal with the United States, as the outgoing Bush administration is eager to leave a legacy where at least in one area — North Korean nuclear proliferation — it will have had a modicum of diplomatic success.

Has North Korea actually made the decision, as Libya did in 2003, to give up completely all its nuclear weapons, materials and facilities, and the ambiguity related to them? After all, it is a program North Korea has been working on for nearly 30 years, over two generations of leaders, and at great cost and risk. For Kim Jong-Il, nuclear weapons are not only an essential security assurance and a bargaining tool, but also an irreplaceable instrument of domestic control and political survival. Although the jury is still out on whether or not North Korea will abandon its nuclear weapons, it is clear that North Korea will want to keep the nuclear weapons and the capabilities to make them for as long as it can.

From the U.S. point of view, a deal with North Korea, even though it is not a perfectly satisfactory one, is better than no deal. The deal freezes the North Korean nuclear program; it gives the United States and others a handle to work on the ultimate and complete denuclearization of North Korea; it gives the United States an opportunity to affect change in the effort to help open North Korean society; and it helps to put a lid on a crisis on the Korean Peninsula. Furthermore, the Bush administration over the years has regarded the Iranian problem as being more serious than North Korea because of its proximity to Israel, presumed relationship with terrorist groups, and its close proximity to oil fields.

In becoming a nuclear weapons state, North Korea has taken advantage of the United States being bogged down in the Middle East, oscillation of U.S. policies, disarray among the regional countries, and a brinkmanship attitude of North Korea that defied risks and dangers. However, economic difficulties, involving especially food and energy shortages, are making it hard for North Korea to continue with its nuclear weapons program. This gives an opening to the international community to denuclearize North Korea, but only if they can effectively calibrate their efforts. It is important and useful to put a lid on the North Korean nuclear issue and program even though it may not lead to a complete resolution of the issue any time soon.

6. Military and Security Challenges

One distinctive fact about the Northeast Asian military balance is that many Asian countries are increasing their defense spending and undertaking large-scale military procurement programs. China is placing an emphasis on expanding its maritime and air power as well as its ballistic missiles capability. China's military modernization since the 1990s owes much to cooperation with Russia on weapons systems and technology. As Russia seems to be having second thoughts about all-out cooperation with China in the military weapons area; and with the U.S. and European arms embargoes since the 1989 Tiananmen Square events broadly in place; China is, in turn, stepping up development of its indigenous military technology. China has a strong interest in building up military capabilities which it can now afford and which are commensurate with its rising economic might. China wishes not only to balance military capabilities of other countries in the region (i.e., Japan and the United States), but also to protect economic activities abroad involving maritime trade routes and energy supplies. China is increasingly in need of global projection capabilities.

In the military area, Japan recognizes the need to respond to the growing military capabilities of China, as well as to effectively support the United States in its global tasks of keeping sea lanes of communication secure and open. Japan also wishes to prepare for contingencies which may arise from regional developments or threats from missile-laden weapons of mass destruction. Japan thus emphasizes new procurements in missile defense, air-refueling tankers, maritime patrol aircraft, combat-aircraft program, and transport aircraft. New equipment brought into service in 2007 included a helicopter-carrying "destroyer," and PAC-3 ballistic-missile defense units. Thus, Japan, which has identified China and North Korea as the main potential threats to its security, has emerged as the world's fifth-largest defense spending country (after the United States, China, the United Kingdom, and France). The series of "reactive" developments in military spending, procurement, and force structure, between China and Japan in particular, may contribute to the emergence of a regional arms race.

Not to be outdone, other regional countries — including North Korea, South Korea, and Taiwan — continue with their military build-up. Pyongyang continues to develop ballistic and other missiles. South Korea increased its defense spending by 9 percent in 2008, and is expected to undertake an annual increase of 6.2 percent under the Defense Reform 2020 program. South Korea's mid-term defense program includes a satellite communications system, airborne early warning aircraft, combat aircraft, a helicopter carrier, and Aegis-equipped destroyer class and air-independent propulsion submarines. The South Korean defense modernization program will get a boost from U.S. government actions that have relaxed sales restrictions on advanced weapons to South Korea. Taiwan is seeking to boost its air combat and missile capability in the face of the People's Liberation Army (PLA) Air Force's growing strength and continuing missile threats.

These developments in the area of military weapons build-up necessitate that the United States enforce four broad sets of actions and policies in order to ensure that an excessive arms race is discouraged and the arms thus procured and acquired are not actually used in armed conflict between and among the regional actors. First, the United States should maintain and strengthen the existing alliance to reassure its allies and friends of the U.S. assistance in case of contingency. Most importantly, the political underpinnings for the alliances should be strengthened. A greater effort should be made by the United States and its allies alike to convince their countrymen and other Asians that the United States is contributing to regional stability and prosperity. Second, it should engage in and encourage confidence building measures (CBMs) between the United States and other regional powers, and between its allies on the one hand and potential adversaries and competitors including China and Russia on the other. Third, it can initiate and engage in arms control dialogue and negotiation with both allies and non-allies alike. Finally, it can try to build a security architecture which involves consultations, coordination, and negotiation on security and strategic matters among various sets of regional countries and powers. Most importantly, strategic dialogue with China, both bilateral and multilateral, would help prevent unnecessary rivalry, competition, and conflict involving China and other countries.

7. East Asian Regional Arrangements

Multilateral organizational arrangements have been a slow and complex business in East Asia. Despite the renewed impetus resulting from the East Asian financial crisis in 1997, East Asian countries have found it difficult to forge new organizational arrangements and to give an institutional form — either on a sub-regional (Northeast Asia) or regional (East Asian) basis — to a de facto community emerging with increasing intra-regional trade, investment, communication, and personnel exchanges. There are several reasons for the difficulty. China-Japan rivalry, both historical and prospective, interferes with achieving the kind of cooperation that existed between France and Germany in the post-World War II period that led to the formation of European community-building. The United States — which had strongly supported European integration during its early period — has remained ambivalent, if not cool, to the prospect of an East Asian community-building in any form. Political-security cooperation in the Asia-Pacific Economic Cooperation (APEC) forum was hampered by the membership of Taiwan and Hong Kong .

The effectiveness of organizations such as the Association of Southeast Asian Nations Plus Three (ASEAN Plus Three) and the East Asian Summit (EAS) have been diminished by the absence of the United States. Various other groupings — such as the three-country high-level meetings of China, Japan, and South Korea; the six-country consultative mechanism to deal with broader regional security issues beyond North Korea's denuclearization; and China-Japan-U.S. consortium to discuss Northeast Asian security and political issues — have a long way to go before becoming a bonafide part of the East Asian regional architecture.

There are two ways in which the United States can actively participate in regional institutional community-making. One is through
direct participation as a bona-fide member in such groupings as
EAS and the Six-Party Talks (as it is doing now). This can be
achieved by being less ambivalent about these organizations, and
meeting some of the "membership" requirements such as joining
the ASEAN Treaty of Amity and Cooperation (TAC). The other is
through encouraging and working closely with its close allies such
as Japan, Australia, and South Korea. These countries are already
core members of some of the other regional organizations and they
will be able to perform the useful and positive task of serving as a
bridge between the "East Asian community" and the United States.

8. Recommendations

1. The United States should maintain its China relations on an
   even keel. It should not repeat the pattern of previous administrations that frequently started out China relations in a rocky
   way only to improve them in later years. The United States
   should take advantage of China's declared intention not to
   upset the status quo and maintain good relations with the
   United States.

2. Even as the United States maintains and strengthens its bilateral
   alliance with its Asian allies, it should engage in multilateral
   security dialogue and building of institutional arrangements
   that will discuss, coordinate, and plan security cooperation and
   coordination.

3. The United States should engage in strategic dialogue, both
   bilateral and multilateral, with key Asian countries — especially

China — not only on trade and security, but also on other matters such as North Korea, proliferation, the environment, and energy resources, particularly natural gas.

4. The United States should sign the Treaty of Amity and Cooperation in Southeast Asia (TAC).

5. Once the TAC is signed, the United States should take a more engaging and open-minded attitude toward regional arrangements in Asia such as the East Asian Summit and ASEAN Plus Three. It can do so by actively participating in those exercises and at the same time encouraging and supporting its allies and friends in Asia to participate in such arrangements and groupings.

6. The United States should show more interest and have more involvement in coping with such global problems as energy resources, environment, and climate change.

7. The United States should initiate and engage in confidence and security building measures with China and Russia; and between them and U.S. allies and friends. They should take measures to prevent an excessive arms race in the region and beyond.

8. Non-proliferation of weapons of mass destruction (WMDs) should be the diplomatic goal of the United States. Regarding the North Korean nuclear program, the next administration would be well advised to continue with the North Korea policy espoused by the Bush administration since the spring of 2007. The United States should also revive and invigorate the Nuclear Nonproliferation Treaty (NPT) system, which has apparently been weakened by several developments including the increased number of de facto nuclear weapons states.

9. The United States Congress should ratify the U.S.-Korea Free Trade Agreement.

10. Even as the United States seeks an early and successful conclusion of the DDA under the World Trade Organization, it should also vigorously negotiate other FTAs with Asian countries; and Congress should ratify FTAs that have already been concluded and signed. The new administration should overcome political constraints in pursuing a win-win game in trade by effectuating liberalization of trade with as many countries as possible.

11. Rather than seeking to be a hegemonic leader in global and regional politics, the United States can be most productive by serving as an effective balancer of power, facilitator of peace and co-existence, broker between adversaries, and guarantor of peace and security.

12. Given the absence of a division of Asia into two or more mutually opposed alliances, and the reluctance of Asians generally to resort to military means to settle disputes, the United States can more productively conduct its relations with Asia by placing greater emphasis on soft power and public diplomacy, which place greater weight on persuasive rather than coercive capabilities.

13. As Asia emerges as the most important region in the world economically, the United States should not only maintain and strengthen its presence in Asia but also pay greater attention to the region. The presence of top U.S. officials including the president, secretary of state, and secretary of defense in Asian or Asia-Pacific gatherings will not only enhance U.S. stature

and influence, but will also be taken as a sign of U.S. attention and involvement in this key region of the world.

14. The United States should be actively involved in building regional architecture in Asia — economic, security, and political. Even as the United States maintains bilateral relations with key countries, it would be well advised to place greater emphasis on multilateral diplomacy and arrangements in economic, security, and political areas.

15. Successive U.S. administrations, including the incumbent Bush administration, have espoused spreading democratic values and enhancing human rights. In recent years, however, in the course of conducting war on terrorism, the United States was seen by many as sometimes being inconsistent with its own principles in dealing with, for example, terrorist suspects and political prisoners abroad. Even in the circumstances of conducting a difficult and dangerous war on terrorism, the United States would be well advised to set a good example by upholding the very values that it espouses.

THE UNITED STATES AND SOUTHEAST ASIA

Tommy Koh

Introduction

The peoples of Southeast Asia are following the 2008 U.S. presidential elections with great attention and admiration, given the open and transparent primary processes. America's real and vibrant democracy is reflected in the competing candidates' travels to every corner of the country to win the hearts and minds of voters. This illustrates that the highest office of the land can neither be secured by wealth nor pedigree and, this year especially, neither race nor gender is an insurmountable obstacle. Consequently, in some parts of the world, including Southeast Asia, anti-Americanism has been balanced by a respect for America's current exercise of democracy.

Confronting a Different World

The 44th president of the United States will inherit a world different from that of his predecessors. After the 1989 fall of the Berlin Wall, during the George H.W. Bush administration, the world made a historic transition from a bipolar to a unipolar one. This, however, was a relatively brief moment in history. By the time President George W. Bush assumed office in January 2001, the world had changed again. A unipolar world had become a multipolar world, with China, India, Russia, Japan – and an enlarged European Union – as new poles. Today, the state of the world is fluid. American scholar Richard Haas has even described it as a nonpolar one. *Newsweek* Foreign Editor Fareed Zakaria's book, "The Post-American World," postulates that America is not necessarily in decline, but other nations — including China, India, and Russia — are rising. In such a multipolar world, he insists, the United States will no longer dominate the global economy and international politics. This scenario presents the next president with many new challenges. How to rebuild trust in America? How to persuade a world to accept American leadership when America is no longer seen as the hegemonic power? How to revive an American economy threatened by recessionary trends? How to defeat terrorists without causing a new Cold War between the West and the Islamic world? How to promote American prosperity without resorting to protectionist measures in the effort to promote a more open global trading system? How to protect American national interests without abandoning America's historic mission of upholding international law, multilateral institutions, and justice in the world?

How America responds to these challenges will determine its future relations with the Asia-Pacific — particularly China, India, Japan, and the Association of Southeast Asian Nations (ASEAN).

Competing for the President's Attention

Although other nations' powers are growing, this does not change the fact that all regions of the world desire America's attention. The United States has the world's largest economy; serves as a security guarantor not only in Asia, but elsewhere; and its cultural influence resonates to varying degress in every corner of the globe. Thus, every region of the world wants America's attention; the only question is whether American attention is positive or negative. Washington's nature is to focus attention on the largest countries, regions, and economies, which can pose a threat to American interest or to international peace and security. By these standards, Southeast Asia — a region largely at peace — does not receive the positive attention it deserves. While the United States may argue that Myanmar (formerly known as Burma) is a toxic influence on the region, Southeast Asia is more at peace than Southeast Europe is. Since the end of the Vietnam War, U.S. attention to Southeast Asia has been episodic rather than consistent, focusing more on security and defense issues. U.S. attention has been less engaged in the dynamics of the region — including economic growth and the development and strengthening of a Southeast Asian regional architecture that is high on the agenda of not only ASEAN, but many Asian nations.

Since the end of the Vietnam War, U.S. attention to Southeast Asia has been episodic rather than consistent, focusing more on security and defense issues. U.S. attention has been less engaged in the dynamics of the region — including economic growth and the development and strengthening of a Southeast Asian regional architecture that is high on the agenda of not only ASEAN, but many Asian nations.

Why is Southeast Asia Important to the United States?

Since the September 11 terrorist attacks, policymakers in Washington have tended to look at Southeast Asia primarily through the unidimensional lens of terrorism. The United States has had a valid concern about terrorist activities in the region. *Jemaah Islamiyah*, the militant Islamic organization based in Southeast Asia and linked to al-Qaeda, has conducted violent operations in Indonesia and the Philippines, and attempted to set off several bombs in Singapore before being thwarted by local authorities. However, since 2002, ASEAN nations have cooperated fully with the United States and each other in sharing intelligence and apprehending Islamic terrorists in the region. This effort has prevented terrorists from launching any major terrorist attack in the region for the past three years. But, there are even more significant reasons why Southeast Asia is important to U.S. political, economic, and security interests. Southeast Asians hope that the next U.S. president will weigh these factors more heavily in the interest of enhancing American prestige and influence in the region.

ASEAN is a more important trade and investment

partner for the United States than Latin America, Russia,

the Middle East, and Africa.

The U.S.-ASEAN economic relationship is substantial, growing, and mutually beneficial. U.S. investment in ASEAN is about US$100 billion, exceeding U.S. investments in China, Hong Kong, and Taiwan combined. U.S. investment in Southeast Asia earns the highest rate of return in the world at approximately 20

percent. The United States is ASEAN's second-largest trading partner and largest foreign direct investor. ASEAN is America's fifth-
largest trading partner and third-largest export market. Few
Americans know that Southeast Asia imports twice as many
American goods as China does. Two-way trade has grown 40 percent since 2001 and amounts to US$170 billion. The United
States has concluded a free trade agreement (FTA) with Singapore
and has attempted to negotiate FTAs with Malaysia and Thailand,
while also concluding bilateral trade and investment framework
agreements (TIFAs) with other ASEAN countries. In sum, ASEAN
is a more important trade and investment partner for the United
States than Latin America, Russia, the Middle East, and Africa.

Since the end of World War II, Southeast Asia has regarded the
United States as a security guarantor of the Asia-Pacific and
welcomes its forward deployed military presence in the region.
America's security presence has ensured that Southeast Asia has not
been dominated by any one power; a core objective of U.S. security
strategy in the region. The United States has bilateral defense
treaties with the Philippines and Thailand and both nations have
been designated as major non-North Atlantic Treaty Organization
(NATO) allies. Singapore allows U.S. air and naval forces access to
its facilities. The United States has also expanded its security relationships with Brunei and Malaysia and resumed full military ties
with Indonesia in 2005 – after more than a decade of sanctions
because of human rights concerns in Timor-Leste, now the world's
newest independent nation.

As the world's preeminent naval power, the United States has benefited from the responsible behavior of Indonesia, Malaysia, and
Singapore for effectively patrolling the Straits of Malacca and
Singapore and their waters in the effort to curb maritime piracy in
the region. The free and safe navigation of these sea lanes is critical

to world commerce and energy transport as more than one-third of global trade and 66 percent of the world's oil and liquefied natural gas passes through the Strait. Energy passing through the Strait of Malacca is three times more than what passes through the Suez Canal and 15 times more than what is transported through the Panama Canal. This is the energy lifeline for China, Japan, and South Korea, as more than 80 percent of its oil and natural gas either comes from or passes through Southeast Asia. In September 2007, the three coastal states (Indonesia, Malaysia, Singapore), the United States, and other user states met in Singapore, under the auspices of the United Nations' International Maritime Organization (IMO); and created a cooperative mechanism to further ensure safe, secure, and efficient shipping in the Straits of Malacca and Singapore.

Americans may be surprised that there are far more Muslims living in Southeast Asia than there are in the Middle East. After more than 45 years of authoritarian rule, Indonesia, the world's most populous Muslim country, has transformed itself over the past decade into a fledgling democracy. The military is no longer Indonesia'a primary political force and efforts to consolidate its democracy have been strengthened through a series of free and fair elections, and economic, legal, and judicial reforms. Hopefully, further consolidation of such reforms will translate into better governance and concrete improvements in the lives of the Indonesian people. The United States should continue to assist Indonesia in its goals for democratic and good governance. Malaysia has also embraced a level of modernity and democracy. Historically, Islam came to Southeast Asia as a result of voluntary rather than forced conversion. Compared with other regions, Islam in Southeast Asia tends to be more accommodating to other religions. Because of the tolerant manner in which Islam is practiced in Southeast Asia, the United States has a much better chance of winning the hearts and minds of Muslims in the region than in any other region of the world.

Energy passing through the Strait of Malacca is three times more

than what passes through the Suez Canal and 15 times more

than what is transported through the Panama Canal. This is the

energy lifeline for China, Japan, and South Korea, as more than

80 percent of its oil and natural gas either comes from or passes

through Southeast Asia

Although Southeast Asian governments were disappointed when senior U.S. officials, including the secretary of state, did not attend important ASEAN meetings, the Bush administation has made efforts to progressively upgrade U.S.-ASEAN relations. In 2002, the United States proposed the Initiative for ASEAN Enterprise to develop FTAs with each Southeast Asian nation, although the requirements may be too steep for ASEAN's weaker economies to adhere to. In 2005, the joint vision statement on the ASEAN-U.S. Enhanced Partnership was signed to provide development opportunities and deepen political, security, economic, and socio-cultural ties throughout Southeast Asia. In 2006, the United States and ASEAN signed the Trade and Investment Framework Agreement (TIFA) to increase trade and investment between our nations. In September 2007, the U.S. Agency for International Development (USAID) approved a budget of up to US$150 million in support of Enhanced Partnership activities. Also in 2007, in a rare display of bi-partisanship, the U.S. Congress, with the support from the Bush administration, adopted legislation to create the new post of U.S. ambassador to ASEAN. Senators Joe Biden (Democrat) and Richard Lugar (Republican), along with other members of the Senate Foreign Relations Committee, should be commended for having taken this initiative. The Bush administration has already appointed an ambassador to this post. The United States is the first Dialogue Partner of ASEAN to have done so and Southeast Asian policymakers are encouraged by this development. Hopefully, the new U.S. ambassador to ASEAN will develop and strengthen U.S. relations with the ASEAN Secretariat and its representatives, including its new Secretary General, Dr. Surin Pitsuwan. The new U.S. administration should be encouraged to post the future U.S. ambassador to ASEAN in Jakarta, where the ASEAN Secretariat is located.

Challenges for U.S.-ASEAN Relations

Despite these positive developments, there is the perception in Southeast Asia that a negative attitude toward ASEAN persists in the United States. A number of U.S. officials regard ASEAN as a talk shop and an ineffectual regional organization. This dismissive attitude is shared by a number of American think-tanks and scholars. This view is mistaken.

Such a perception is due partly to the fact that the United States prefers to deal bilaterally with each ASEAN nation. In one respect, this is understandable because the U.S. enjoys more leverage in bilateral negotiations than in a multilateral setting. The U.S. wants quick results, but multilateral meetings are complicated as diverse nations have diverse interests. Moreover, given the four-year cycle and overall structure of America's political system, the U.S. does not tend to take a long-term view of policy. Thus, the United States gives the impression that it is not willing to nurture relationships with nascent institutions which may not produce immediate results, and that it is not willing to show its Asian interlocutors respect. For American officials, a meeting may not be worth attending unless it has a concrete deliverable. This could explain the absence of senior U.S. officials from some important ASEAN meetings over the past four years.

The United States gives the impression that it is not willing to nurture relationships with nascent institutions which may not produce immediate results, and that it is not willing to show its Asian interlocutors respect.

This negative U.S. attitude is also based on an inadequate knowledge of what ASEAN has achieved over the decades and its usefulness to the U.S. There are three examples that can substantiate this point.

First, following the disaster inflicted on Myanmar by the Nargis cyclone, the world was anxious to help, but the rulers of Myanmar were suspicious of the intentions of Western countries. Myanmar generals feared that under the cover of humanitarian relief, some Western countries (particularly the U.S.) had a political agenda, which included regime change. They also felt threatened by European rhetoric, suggesting that, under the doctrine of responsibility to protect (R2P), aid could be delivered to the victims without the consent of the affected country. The impasse between Myanmar and the international community was overcome by ASEAN. The current chairman of ASEAN, Singapore's Foreign Minister George Yeo, convened a special meeting of ASEAN's foreign ministers on May 19, 2008, which enabled ASEAN to persuade the Government of Myanmar to accept humanitarian assistance, to empower ASEAN to take the lead, and to agree for ASEAN and the United Nations to co-chair a pledging conference in Yangon on May 25th. As a result of ASEAN's initiative, the door was opened and foreign assistance and relief workers started to arrive. While no one will argue the situation in Myanmar is ideal, it is incomparably better than the two-week period after Cyclone Nargis struck, when humanitarian assistance could not reach the 2.5 million people (half who are women and children) in the Irrawaddy Delta.

Washington seems to not understand or appreciate the important role ASEAN plays as the region's facilitator, convenor, and peacemaker. After the Cold War, ASEAN took two thoughtful initiatives. The first initiative was to welcome its three former adversaries — Vietnam, Laos, and Cambodia — into ASEAN; it also invited Myanmar, a county that isolated itself from the world for more than three decades. Many outside the region, particularly Americans, have been critical of ASEAN for including its newest members in the grouping, saying their levels of economic and political development are much lower than the original members. ASEAN, however, believes that by integrating its newer members, it will ultimately strengthen the region and ensure peace, development, and economic prosperity.

The second initiative was much bolder and led to the founding of the ASEAN Regional Forum (ARF), a 26-member security roundtable that, in addition to the ASEAN nations, includes the United States, China, Japan, India, and Russia. Together, all of these nations have a stake in the peace and stability of the Asia-Pacific. Since 1994, ARF has become the principal forum for security dialogue in Asia, complementing various bilateral alliances and dialogues. It provides a setting in which members can discuss regional security issues and develop cooperative measures to enhance and ensure peace and security throughout the Asia-Pacific. While confidence building measures have been set in place, efforts are ongoing to develop the tools of preventive diplomacy and conflict management. The ARF has the potential to become the Asian equivalent of the Organization for Security and Cooperation in Europe (OSCE); but for this to happen, a secretariat for ARF would need to be created.

Washington seems to not understand or appreciate the

important role ASEAN plays as the region's facilitator,

convenor, and peacemaker.

The 1997 Asian Financial Crisis taught Asians several valuable lessons. The Thais learned they could not rely on the United States to assist them, as Thailand is less important to the U.S. than, for example, Mexico. For the Japanese, the lesson was that the U.S. and Europe would not permit Japan to launch an Asian monetary fund which could potentially rival the International Monetary Fund (IMF). Finally, Asians throughout the region learned that the fate of Southeast Asia and Northeast Asia is intertwined when the

fall of the Thai *baht* ricocheted northwards and brought down the
Korean *won*. This new insight created the ASEAN Plus Three
framework and led ASEAN to convene the first ASEAN Plus
Three (China, Japan, and Korea) Summit in 1997. The ASEAN
Plus Three process has endured and proved to be a very useful
forum. It launched the Chiang Mai Initiative, which has brought
together the finance ministers and central banks of the 13 countries to promote better surveillance, macro-economic coordination,
and currency swaps. Because of ASEAN Plus Three, three
Northeast Asian leaders met together for the first time in 1997.
At this juncture, ASEAN Plus Three is exploring the feasibility of
concluding an ASEAN Plus Three Free Trade Agreement. If this
FTA is created, it would represent the world's largest free trade
area, comprising a population of two billion (one-third of humanity)
and a combined gross national product of $15 trillion.

*The East Asia Summit is strategically important because, apart
from ASEAN, it includes Asia's three major powers: China, India,
and Japan. ASEAN's aspiration is to embed them in a cooperative
mechanism, thereby reducing misunderstanding and suspicion
among them and enhancing the prospects of peace in Asia.*

In 2005, ASEAN launched another initiative and convened the
first East Asia Summit, involving the leaders of ASEAN Plus Three
plus Australia, India, and New Zealand. The logic of this larger
grouping is based upon geography and shared interests. It is also

based on the economic logic that, largely driven by the private sector, intra-East Asian trade now constitutes 55 percent of the region's trade with the world. The East Asia Summit is strategically important because, apart from ASEAN, it includes Asia's three major powers: China, India, and Japan. ASEAN's aspiration is to embed them in a cooperative mechanism, thereby reducing misunderstanding and suspicion among them and enhancing the prospects of peace in Asia. The East Asia Summit has recently started to focus on the important issues of energy security, climate change, and environmental sustainability. How Asia addresses these issues and cooperates together in future decades is critical to the development and environmental sustainability of Southeast Asia and the entire Asia-Pacific region. There are many American skeptics who believe that creating an effective East Asian Community is not possible. Time will tell and the process will not materialize overnight. But, an East Asian Community is a natural desire in the region to forge ties and create a stronger regional identity. It would be myopic for the United States to underestimate this desire. If the U.S. takes a narrow perspective on this issue, it stands to lose influence in the region. Many Asian countries share a suspicion that the U.S. does not want to see Asia become integrated. Even if the U.S. is not part of the East Asia Community, it would still be important for the grouping to engage with the U.S. as a dialogue partner. Any discussion about how to solve global challenges — from environmental degradation, energy security, infectious diseases, transnational crime, and natural disasters to trade, finance, and investment — must include the United States. Since the end of the Cold War, much of the world, including Asia, acknowledges that the U.S. is a great power. What Asians are questioning now is whether the U.S. can be an effective leader in an era when other nations are increasing their power and influence in Southeast Asia and elsewhere.

What Asians are questioning now is whether the U.S. can be an effective leader in an era when other nations are increasing their power and influence in Southeast Asia and elsewhere.

Other Suitors

The new U.S. president should be aware that Southeast Asia has many suitors besides the United States. ASEAN has already concluded free trade agreements with China, the Republic of Korea and Japan, and is negotiating such agreements with India, Australia, New Zealand, and the European Union. The United States used to be the region's largest trading partner. This distinction now belongs to China.

Recommendations and Conclusions: An Agenda for the Next U.S. President

Over the past few years, the United States has been adjusting to the expectation to act more multilaterally. Multilateralism cannot be a substitute for bilateralism, but multilateralism can complement bilateralism. Together they are far better than the unilateralism pursued by the United States earlier this decade. The next president of the United States has the opportunity to improve and strengthen relations with Southeast Asia by doing the following.

1. America's next president should hold a summit meeting with the leaders of ASEAN. ASEAN has held such summits with

Japan, China, India, and other dialogue partners but not with the United States. Summit meetings may or may not achieve much in substance but they bear a strong political signature. It is a way for the United States to illustrate that it values Southeast Asia and ASEAN as a regional organization.

2. The United States should sign the ASEAN Treaty of Amity and Cooperation (TAC). The TAC contains, *inter alia*, six principles governing relations between states. The principles are based on those in the UN Charter — such as non-interference in the internal affairs of one another, and the peaceful settlement of disputes — and requires consensus in the decisionmaking process. There is nothing in the TAC that the United States has not previously subscribed to. The TAC has been signed by China, Japan, Korea, India, Australia, New Zealand, Russia, France, and the United Kingdom, among others. The U.S. is the odd man out. Ideally, after careful preparation, the TAC could be signed at the first ever U.S.-ASEAN summit.

The United States should sign the ASEAN Treaty of Amity and Cooperation (TAC). ...There is nothing in the TAC that the United States has not previously subscribed to. The TAC has been signed by China, Japan, Korea, India, Australia, New Zealand, Russia, France, and the United Kingdom, among others. The U.S. is the odd man out.

---

3. The United States should be more proactive in nurturing the ASEAN Regional Forum (ARF) and helping it make the necessary transition from confidence building to preventive diplomacy. The United States has recently proposed the idea of developing a standing coordinating mechanism to respond to humanitarian emergencies, such as the tsunami in 2004, the recent cyclone in Myanmar, and the earthquake in China's Sichuan province. This is a good and timely proposal and would enjoy the support of all ARF members. It is hoped that the next U.S. administration will act on this proposal.

4. The U.S. and ASEAN should begin a new dialogue on energy security and climate change. The next U.S. administration and ASEAN should cooperate to bring the Bali roadmap on climate change and greenhouse gas emissions to a successful conclusion. Some of the ASEAN countries are richly endowed with oil and gas resources. They are also home to some of the largest remaining tropical rain forests in the world. It would be greatly appreciated if the United States could support the "Heart of Borneo" project — proposed jointly by Brunei, Indonesia, and Malaysia — which aims to conserve one of the largest remaining tropical rain forests in the world. The United States is the world's largest emitter of greenhouse gases. It has to join the European Union and Japan in agreeing to substantial reductions of its carbon dioxide emissions. ASEAN nations would also benefit if the United States would share its expertise in energy efficiency, clean and renewable energy, carbon capture and sequestration, and other technologies.

5. ASEAN hopes the next U.S. president will uphold America's commitment to globalization, free trade, and international rules. Although the United States is the biggest beneficiary of globalization, there are sections of the American public that are

opposed to and feel threatened by globalization. Asians are concerned by the anti-free trade rhetoric of some of the candidates during the presidential primary. In the last decade, there has been a noticeable retreat by America from its historic commitment to international rules. The global economy would receive a lift if the next administration worked toward a successful conclusion of the Doha Development Round of multilateral trade negotiations under the auspices of the World Trade Organization. It would be very helpful if the U.S. Congress would empower the new president with fast-track authority.

ASEAN hopes the next U.S. president will uphold America's commitment to globalization, free trade, and international rules... Asians are concerned by the anti-free trade rhetoric of some of the candidates during the presidential primary.

---

6. Both the public and private sectors in the United States and Southeast Asia should consider the feasibility of launching a major initiative to help ASEAN countries improve their infrastructure – highways, ports, communication networks, power grids, and other components. This would require action on both sides. On the ASEAN side, domestic laws and policies should be reformed and codified to make it possible and attractive for the U.S. private sector to participate. On the U.S. side, the government should work with the U.S.-ASEAN Business Council, the World Bank, and the Asian Development Bank.

7. The United States and ASEAN should intensify their cooperation in the whole spectrum of non-traditional security challenges, such as Avian Flu, HIV/AIDS, malaria, and other threats to public health; as well as work more closely in combating drugs and human trafficking, maritime piracy, natural disaster and humanitarian emergencies; and promote food security at a time when food prices are soaring and there is a need to double the world's food production over the next 30 years.

8. The new administration should respond in constructive ways to the rise of Asia, especially China and India. ASEAN would like the United States to continue to deal with China as a responsible stakeholder and not as an adversary; it would also not welcome any attempt by the U.S. to play China and India off against each other.

ASEAN would like the United States to continue to deal with China as a responsible stakeholder and not as an adversary; it would also not welcome any attempt by the U.S. to play China and India off against each other.

---

9. America's interests would be better served in Southeast Asia (and elsewhere) if it exercised its public diplomacy more effectively. It was a blunder for America to have downgraded the old U.S. Information Agency (USIA) and the various American centers in Asia to small "American Corners" where Southeast

Asians no can longer interface with representatives of the American diplomatic community — nor scholars, writers, artists, musicians, and other individuals who contribute so richly to American culture and society. We urge the new administration to consider a new program of building cultural, artistic, and intellectual bridges between America and the countries and peoples of Southeast Asia. This should include civil society organizations, women, and young people.

10. The United States and ASEAN should consider establishing a Group of Eminent Persons, to take stock of U.S.-ASEAN relations and to make recommendations for elevating those relations to a higher and more strategic level. The creation of such a grouping could assist greatly in framing the agenda for a U.S.-ASEAN summit and in determining how the United States can sign the Treaty of Amity and Cooperation.

This is a pivotal moment in ASEAN's development as it strives to create a comprehensive regional plan that encompasses economic, social, and political issues for all. It has adopted the ASEAN Economic Community Blueprint which would, by 2015, transform Southeast Asia's 10 national economies into a single market and production base with free flows of good, services, capital, and skilled labor. It has also adopted the ASEAN Charter, which would make ASEAN a more rules-based organization, strengthen its adherence to human rights and democracy, and establish an ASEAN Human Rights Body. No one is denying that the tragic situation in Myanmar is important, but the wider prospects of regional programs should not be held hostage to it. American policymakers should bear in mind that the ASEAN Charter is a milestone, not a destination, in the region's effort to foster peace, stability, development, and economic prosperity.

Americans should also bear in mind that ASEAN, after the European Union, is probably the world's most vibrant regional organization. At a time when America's friendships in the region are questioned due to its policies in Iraq and elsewhere in the Middle East, the United States must think twice about missing opportunities to show Southeast Asians that the U.S. views it more positively than just another front in the war against terrorism. It is important for the United States to become more engaged with ASEAN and Southeast Asians on a broad agenda. The recommendations articulated above can contribute to this effort. If this can be accomplished, the future of U.S.-ASEAN relations will be positive and to the benefit of all.

THE U.S. ROLE IN SOUTH ASIA

C. Raja Mohan

After years of relative marginalization, South Asia is steadily increasing its influence in international affairs. All major powers, including the United States, European Union, China, Japan, and Russia, are expanding their engagement with the Subcontinent. On the economic front, India's high level of performance in recent years has brought the region into sharp focus. However, such high growth rates are also visible across the Subcontinent, making it the second-fastest growing region in the world — after China. India is now an important factor in managing new international trade, energy, and environmental challenges. On the political front, most major issues that confront U.S. policy — international terrorism, Islamic radicalism, weapons of mass destruction, proliferation, state failure, nation building, and promotion of democracy — are ingrained in the South Asian Subcontinent. South Asia will become increasingly relevant to a number of new challenges confronting U.S. foreign policy, such as Asia's regional balance of power, maritime security, and global warming. South Asia is at the crossroads of a rising Asia, making its geopolitical relevance significant. Strengthening the U.S. partnership with all the South Asian countries is likely to have positive spillover effects in East Asia, the former Soviet republics of Central Asia, the Middle East, and Africa. A strong Subcontinent, in harmony with itself and engaged with the United States, can emerge as a force for peace and stability across the Indian Ocean and its littoral.

Since the late 1990s, the United States has devoted considerable political and diplomatic energies to its engagement with South

Asia, which developed a new intensity after September 11, 2001. These bipartisan efforts have produced a number of positive results — including producing a credible framework for an enduring strategic partnership with India, the centerpiece of which has been the historic civil nuclear initiative. Also, in the last few years, the United States has simultaneously helped to improve bilateral relations between New Delhi and Islamabad, an objective that for decades was deemed impossible. Deliberate American neutrality in the India-Pakistan conflicts has encouraged New Delhi and Islamabad to embark on a bilateral, and rather productive, peace process. Since 9/11, America has been involved in stabilizing Pakistan and Afghanistan against local and trans-national threats of terrorism and religious extremism, while also economically modernizing the region. Consequently, the United States has emerged as the single-most important external partner of the Subcontinent. Although America's recent gains in South Asia are indeed historic, they remain to be consolidated. There also exists the danger that some of the U.S. advances in the region might be reversed in the near future.

This chapter defines five broad objectives for the next administration's approach toward South Asia and 10 specific policy recommendations.

THE OBJECTIVES

1. Regain the initiative in the War on Terror

The principal security threats to the United States today are rooted in the re-entrenchment of al-Qaeda in the border regions between Pakistan and Afghanistan. The U.S. pursuit of the war against al-Qaeda has been complicated by the emerging instabilities in Afghanistan and Pakistan. Amidst the U.S. difficulties to mobilize a more effective North Atlantic Treaty Organization (NATO) participation in the stabilization of Afghanistan, a strategic failure there is no longer beyond the realm of imagination. The next administration needs to develop a comprehensive strategy that seeks to overcome the many political hurdles blocking success in the war on terror. These challenges include the Karzai government's inability to reverse the Pushtun tribes' disaffection (which contributes to the re-emergence of the Taliban and al-Qaeda), the enduring contradictions between the national interests of Pakistan and Afghanistan, the lack of ownership of the war on terror among the civilian leaders in Pakistan, and the temptation of Pakistan's civilian government to create short-term political deals which can strengthen the militant groups, the Taliban, and al-Qaeda in the long run.

Amidst the U.S. difficulties to mobilize a more effective North Atlantic Treaty Organization (NATO) participation in the stabilization of Afghanistan, a strategic failure there is no longer beyond the realm of imagination. The next administration needs to develop a comprehensive strategy that seeks to overcome the many political hurdles blocking success in the war on terror.

---

2. Deepen U.S.-India relations

Recently, improving ties with India has been an important strategic priority for the United States. Washington's bipartisan approach to India is reflected in the Democratic Party's leadership and in the Republican Bush administration's decision to renew civilian nuclear cooperation with India. As the government in New Delhi copes with fierce political resistance from the Indian communist parties to the civil nuclear initiative and the transformation of Indo-U.S. relations, Washington has shown necessary patience. The next administration, however, must resist the temptation to renegotiate the nuclear agreement with India. The original, principal objectives of the nuclear initiative were to integrate India into the management of the global nuclear order, remove the long accumulated mutual political distrust between Washington and New Delhi over the nuclear issue, and create the basis for a stronger bilateral partnership. That precisely is the reason why the Indian communist parties want to see the deal's demise. The next administration must reaffirm the commitment for an early implementation of the civil nuclear initiative with India. Simultaneously, it must find ways to insulate the promising parts of the relationship — especially defense cooperation — if the absence of a political consensus in India delays the implementation of the civil nuclear initiative. The next U.S. administration must persist with the core objectives of transforming bilateral relations with India.

3. Respond to China's rise in South Asia

American primacy on the Subcontinent is in danger of being compromised by the steady expansion of Chinese influence in the region. For example, U.S. trade with India grew from US$14 billion in 2000 to US$41 billion in 2007. In the same period, China's trade with India grew from US$3 billion to nearly US$38 billion. This trend applies to China's trade with the entire region; Beijing is likely to emerge as the largest trading partner of all South Asian nations in the near future. For nearly a decade, China has relentlessly pressed ahead with a grand plan to link western China with the Subcontinent through rail and road networks. This overland effort comes at a time when China is seeking to expand its maritime capability and is actively involved in constructing maritime infrastructure in Pakistan, Sri Lanka, Bangladesh, and Myanmar (formerly known as Burma). South Asia and its waters have become critical for Beijing's strategic calculus on energy security and the development of its Western regions. A purposeful U.S. policy toward South Asia would not only constrain Chinese plans to convert its new economic presence in the region into strategic clout; but also help restore the Subcontinent's influence in China's Xinjiang, Tibet and Yunnan provinces, which traditionally have been parts of the Subcontinent's hinterland.

The next administration, however, must resist the temptation to renegotiate the nuclear agreement with India. The original, principal objectives of the nuclear initiative were to integrate India into the management of the global nuclear order, remove the long accumulated mutual political distrust between Washington and New Delhi over the nuclear issue, and create the basis for a stronger bilateral partnership.

---

4. Promote regional economic integration

The core of any U.S. strategy toward the region must be a commitment to accelerate the unfolding integration of the South Asian economies. After years of lackadaisical regionalism, South Asia is now moving toward the implementation of a free trade area, signaling its new outward orientation. The South Asian Association for Regional Cooperation (SAARC), the Subcontinent's only collective forum, has recently admitted the United States, China, Japan, South Korea, and the European Union as observers. The SAARC has also admitted Afghanistan as a full member, in an expansion of its regional footprint. It is in the U.S. interest to see the rapid emergence of an economic community in South Asia that could eventually rival China's size, dynamism, and global impact. A strong and economically integrated South Asia can reclaim its historic role in promoting stability and the balance of power in the Middle East, Central Asia, and Southeast Asia. Working with Japan and the European Union, the United States. should encourage SAARC initiatives on global warming, energy security and efficiency, and education.

It is in the U.S. interest to see the rapid emergence of an economic community in South Asia that could eventually rival China's size, dynamism, and global impact. A strong and economically integrated South Asia can reclaim its historic role in promoting stability and the balance of power in the Middle East, Central Asia, and Southeast Asia.

---

5. Leverage American soft power

Given its recent preoccupation with the global war on terror, the United States has tended to undervalue its broader range of equities on the Subcontinent. Despite resentment in many quarters about the recent thrust of its policies, the United States has nonetheless developed a huge reservoir of goodwill in the Subcontinent. The United States needs to find ways to synergize its pursuit of its interests with its enduring cultural attractiveness on the Subcontinent. Promoting democracy has been a major thrust of U.S. policy in recent years, but democracy's implementation in the Subcontinent has been beset with multiple contradictions. For example, the U.S has demanded the complete isolation of the military rulers in Burma; yet in Pakistan, the U.S. has wavered between its commitment to promoting democracy and retaining its leverage with the Pakistani Army, which has traditionally dominated the polity. In Nepal, the U.S.'s narrow emphasis on counter-terrorism has overlooked the Maoists' importance as a political force representing long-overdue social and political modernization. Since 1996, the Maoists have taken arms in demanding various reforms, which included the replacement of the monarchy with a republic. While their use of violence against innocent people in pursuit of their political aims were among good reasons for the United States to label the Maoists as a terrorist organization, there is also the larger imperative of drawing them into the political mainstream. The Maoists emerged as the single-largest political formation in the elections to the Constituent Assembly in early 2008.

More broadly, the South Asian political elites admire the core political values of the western world — including the tradition of common law, administrative systems, financial and banking cultures, and the English language. These intellectual bonds distinguish the Subcontinent from much of East Asia and the Middle

East. U.S. foreign policy needs to take full advantage of this shared culture by significantly expanding its public diplomacy in South Asia. Easing the U.S. visa regulations for South Asian professionals will help build lasting ties between America and the Subcontinent.

The United States needs to find ways to synergize its pursuit of its interests with its enduring cultural attractiveness on the Subcontinent. Promoting democracy has been a major thrust of U.S. policy in recent years, but democracy's implementation in the Subcontinent has been beset with multiple contradictions.

POLICY RECOMMENDATIONS

1. Unveil a long-term military commitment to Afghanistan

Throughout South Asia, there is widespread political assumption that the U.S. commitment to nation building in Afghanistan is, at best, a short-term one. This, in turn, leaves no real incentive for key players in the region to take political decisions that conform to U.S. objectives. The new administration needs to lend some teeth to its 2005 declaration on a strategic partnership with Afghanistan by unveiling a bilateral defense treaty. This would signal a significant American military presence for the foreseeable future. If the United States prepares to draw down its forces in Iraq in the coming years, it should be in a position to enhance U.S. troop presence in Afghanistan. A stronger U.S. military commitment, however, is not enough. It must be supplemented by a range of other measures that streamline the current chaotic international involvement in Afghanistan and enhance Afghanistan's national capacity to sustain its own military and police forces. Instead of the current emphasis in Washington on the scale, scope, and depth of NATO's commitment to Afghanistan's stabilization, the United States should concentrate on altering the regional political dynamic in and around the Pakistan-Afghanistan border.

If the United States prepares to draw down its forces in Iraq in the coming years, it should be in a position to enhance U.S. troop presence in Afghanistan.

---

2. Engage the Pushtun tribes

The most important terrorist threat to the United States stems from a single ethnic community, the Pushtuns, who straddle across the Durand Line – the 1893-drawn border between Pakistan and Afghanistan. There are nearly 25 million Pushtuns in Pakistan and 15 million in Afghanistan. Without significant cooperation from the Pushtun tribes on both sides of the Durand Line, the United States will find it near impossible to defeat the Taliban and al-Qaeda. A counter-terror strategy focused only on hunting extremists by attacking Pushtun territories is likely to inflame anti-American sentiment among the tribes and draw them closer to al-Qaeda and the Taliban. The United States must undertake a significant effort to win political support among the Pushtun tribes, sep-

arate them from al-Qaeda and the Taliban, and make them stakeholders in the war against terror. The United States must help the
Pakistani and Afghan governments strengthen the traditional
Pushtun tribal structures. The United States also needs to recognize
how deeply the Pushtun question divides Pakistan and
Afghanistan. To prevent Pushtun ethnic nationalism from undermining Pakistan's territorial unity and integrity, Pakistani governments have long promoted religious radicalism in the tribal areas.
The U.S. interest, on the other hand, is to separate Pushtun tribes
from extremists. This core contradiction between the interests of
Washington and Islamabad cannot be resolved without addressing
the Pakistan-Afghanistan dispute over the Durand Line.

3. Transform the Durand Line

Since Pakistan's birth in 1947, Kabul has been at odds with
Islamabad. Afghanistan refused to recognize Pakistan as a succes-
sor state to the British Raj and the Durand Line as the legitimate
border. That the British drew the Durand Line across Pushtun territories and imposed it on a weak Kabul is a major national griev-
ance in Afghanistan; no political formation in Afghanistan,
including the Taliban, is willing to accept the Durand Line as the
legitimate border with Pakistan. Islamabad, on the other hand,
cannot afford to redraw the boundary with Afghanistan. Any
long-term reconciliation between Pakistan and Afghanistan would
necessarily involve a broad understanding on transforming the
Durand Line without redrawing it. The United States can do this
by getting Islamabad and Kabul to accept a new set of principles
— which meets Pakistan's desire for a secure western frontier and
Kabul's demand for an end to Pakistan's forward policy in
Pushtun areas — through helping to create cross-border institutions that facilitate greater cooperation among the Pushtun tribes.
Agreements between Kabul and Islamabad, supported by

Washington, must include a commitment not to change the Durand Line by force, facilitate easy movement of tribes that overlap the border, and mutual cooperation to prevent hostile movement of extremists. The United States also needs a bold plan that builds on the current initiatives for a joint trans-border *jirga*; military consultations between international forces, Afghan National Army and Pakistani security forces; and plans for cross-frontier reconstruction opportunity zones. This would involve a more ambitious strategy for the development of tribal areas on both sides of the Durand Line. Such a strategy must recall the traditional role of the Pushtun lands as a bridge between the Subcontinent on the one hand, and Central Asia and the Gulf on the other. Any restoration of trans-frontier commerce in the region would mean supporting a framework for trilateral coopera-tion between Afghanistan, Pakistan, and India.

4. Promote India-Pakistan-Afghanistan cooperation

Pakistan's sense of a rivalry with India in Afghanistan has been an enduring element of Islamabad's security anxieties. Mutual antago-nism toward Pakistan has tended to draw New Delhi and Kabul closer over the decades. The United States has an opportunity to break this old pattern. Since 2004, India and Pakistan have sustained a productive peace process, which provides a new basis for ameliorating India-Pakistan rivalry in Afghanistan. India is increasingly aware that it cannot sustain its activism in Afghanistan in the face of Pakistan's hostility. Islamabad, on the other hand, needs to acknowledge that it cannot unilaterally shape the political evolution of Afghanistan. Washington should support the idea of an annual trilateral summit between the top leaders of Afghanistan, Pakistan, and India to focus on economic cooperation and counter-terrorism. The United States should encourage all three countries to negotiate a liberal trade and transit treaty that will allow Kabul access to the larger Indian market, New Delhi to gain overland access to Afghanistan and Central Asia via Pakistan, and Islamabad to benefit from large volumes of transit trade. The regions between Kabul and Delhi were once part of a single economic space. Its reconstitution will provide a regional core that could complement U.S. objectives of stabilizing and modernizing the north-western parts of the Subcontinent.

5. Support India-Pakistan reconciliation in Kashmir

Promoting India-Pakistan reconciliation and encouraging a solution to the dispute over Jammu and Kashmir has been a longstanding objective of the United States. However, attempts by the United States to directly impose itself between the two have tended to be counterproductive. A more detached U.S. policy toward the Kashmir question in recent years, however, has created the space for India and Pakistan to embark on a substantive dialogue on the intractable dispute. While the two sides have made considerable progress in drafting a new framework for the resolution of the Kashmir question, Islamabad's inability or unwillingness to restrain the Kashmir militants based on its soil may yet lead to an unraveling of the peace process. Just as the United States is concerned with Islamabad's new efforts to placate militant groups, India too is apprehensive that Pakistan might be backsliding on its commitment to control cross-border terrorism. It is in the U.S. interest that the civilian leaders of Pakistan stay the course laid down by President Pervez Musharraf on restraining cross-border terrorism and taking new steps towards a final settlement in Kashmir. A consolidation of the peace process in Kashmir and tranquility on the India-Pakistan frontier will allow Islamabad to address the new challenges to its security on its western borders and lend more effective support to the U.S. war on terror.

6. Reduce the salience of Pakistan's nuclear arsenal

Pakistan offers two important challenges to U.S. non-proliferation policy. One is A.Q. Khan's proliferation network, discovered earlier this decade. Many in the United States — and the world — remain skeptical over Islamabad's assertion that Dr. Khan was acting on his own and that the network has since been disabled. Recently, Dr. Khan asserted that he was coerced into making his confession and that the Pakistani Army and other officials were involved in the Pakistan-centered proliferation network. The Bush administration has avoided a public debate on the issue. The next administration needs to undertake a comprehensive review of the A.Q. Khan affair and reassess Pakistan's role in the nuclear black market. A second concern for the United States stems from the security and safety of Pakistan's nuclear arsenal; it appears that Pakistan's Army maintains tight control over it. This, however, could change if Pakistan spirals into an unpredictable crisis. The United States has already taken a number of steps to assist Pakistan in securing its control over nuclear weapons; however, technical solutions to the security and safety of Pakistan's nuclear arsenal are not enough. As long as Pakistan's nuclear arsenal exists and the danger of state failure in Pakistan seems real, there is no assurance that nuclear weapons will not fall into the hands of extremist groups. Over the longer term, the United States needs to address Pakistan's broader security imperatives that prompted the very construction and maintenance of its nuclear weapons. A consolidation of the India-Pakistan rapprochement, together with reconciliation with Afghanistan, would let Pakistan secure its territorial frontiers and lessen the salience of nuclear weapons in its security calculus. This will involve encouraging the Pakistan Army to rethink its traditional approach to national security. This, in turn, would require a re-definition of civil-military relations in Pakistan in favor of the elected governments.

A consolidation of the India-Pakistan rapprochement, together with reconciliation with Afghanistan, would let Pakistan secure its territorial frontiers and lessen the salience of nuclear weapons in its security calculus.

7. Seek freer trade with and within South Asia

Amidst an acceleration of region-wide growth and the real prospects for eliminating mass poverty, the Subcontinent needs a strong economic partnership with the United States. With the U.S. becoming an observer at the SAARC, the region's economic expectations of the U.S. have sharply increased. Even the smaller countries in South Asia are no longer looking toward traditional forms of U.S. aid, but want opportunities for trade, foreign direct investment, and open markets. An American drift toward protectionism will harm South Asia's economic growth and push it deeper into China's economic political orbit. Washington can help accelerate the process of regional economic integration by offering preferential tariffs to goods produced across borders in South Asia, and encourage investments by its companies on the Subcontinent. As the region moves toward a free trade area and seeks trans-border connections, the United States can raise its influence in the region by supporting region-wide projects for economic development, energy transfers, and trans-border transportation corridors.

With the U.S. becoming an observer at the SAARC, the region's economic expectations of the U.S. have sharply increased. Even the smaller countries in South Asia are no longer looking toward traditional forms of U.S. aid, but want opportunities for trade, foreign direct investment, and open markets.

8. Support transregional infrastructure projects

The United States formally supports South Asia's integration with its abutting regions, especially Southeast Asia and Central Asia. Yet, the U.S. has come down hard against the region's expanding economic cooperation with Myanmar and Iran. The U.S. needs to rethink this policy. Traditionally, both these nations were very much part of British India's sphere of influence. Encouraging an India-led SAARC to regain a measure of influence in both Myanmar and Iran might be in the longer-term interests of the United States. Stronger cooperation between South Asia and Burma will serve to balance China's expanding influence there. That greater external pressure might only harden the xenophobic attitudes in Myanmar has been confirmed by the regime's refusal to allow substantive international assistance to the victims of Cyclone Nargis in May 2008. A more credible strategy toward Myanmar might involve Western reassurances on the unity and territorial integrity of the nation and promises of significant international assistance in stages in return for a genuine road-map on internal political liberalization. The United States must encourage SAARC and the Association of Southeast Asian Nations (ASEAN) to nudge Myanmar to open its economy and society by becoming a land bridge between the Subcontinent and Southeast Asia.

As the next administration reviews its policies toward Iran, Washington must either lift its opposition to the India-Pakistan-Iran (IPI) pipeline or propose alternatives that will allow South Asia to meet its energy requirements. One alternative to the IPI pipeline is the Asian Development Bank-funded TAPI pipeline involving Turkmenistan, Afghanistan, Pakistan, and India. The other involves the construction of an underwater pipeline from the Arab Gulf to the Subcontinent. To manage the rising influence of Iran, the United States also needs to encourage stronger economic, political, and security cooperation between SAARC and the Gulf Cooperation Council. As Iraq slowly stabilizes, the United States should welcome greater South Asian participation in the country's economic reconstruction.

9. Strengthen civil society in the region

Unlike some parts of East Asia and much of the Middle East, the Subcontinent is defined by an irrepressible civil society. Across the Subcontinent, non-governmental organizations thrive to provide a measure of balance against excessive dominance by state structures. Any long-term U.S. strategy that aims to leverage its soft power in the region must focus on engaging civil society. It would involve a renewed outreach to South Asian Muslims, who have traditionally been moderate in their political orientation and deeply embedded in the eclectic culture of the Subcontinent. American engagement with South Asian Muslims is crucial as 40 percent of the world's Muslims live on the Subcontinent. While the Indian diaspora has made its mark in the western world, the diasporas from Pakistan,

Bangladesh, and elsewhere are equally accomplished and provide an important link between the United States and South Asia. South Asian elites, as well as many in the lower middle class, highly value modern education as a critical resource for their future generations. The U.S. needs a massive public-private partnership between American institutions and those in South Asia to meet the huge shortfall in the supply of education and training at all levels. The U.S. should avoid visa restrictions against South Asian middle classes that are natural allies of the west.

10. Expand India's role in global governance

Recent U.S. efforts to transform relations with India are driven by larger considerations of global governance. The United States recognizes the importance of a rising India in the reconstruction of international institutions. While the U.S. has often talked about making India a full partner in the management of the global order, it is yet to take definitive steps. The expansion of the permanent membership of the United Nations no longer seems a practical proposition in the near term. The next administration must initiate immediate steps to make India a full member of the G-8 group of advanced nations. On new global issues that confront the world today — such as controlling carbon emissions or the management of the challenges on energy, resource, and food security — India has now emerged as a decisive player. Any attempt by the United States to force India to comply with a new set of norms might be counterproductive. No government in India would be prepared to abandon the objective of promoting the economic well-being of its billion-plus population.

For the United States, the operative principle is a simple one: to think and travel together with India in the construction of a new international system, rather than demanding that New Delhi "prove" itself to be a stakeholder. This would mean making India a full partner in the writing of new rules for institutions that accommodate a rapidly changing world.

The next administration must initiate immediate steps to make India a full member of the G-8 group of advanced nations. On new global issues that confront the world today — such as controlling carbon emissions or the management of the challenges on energy, resource, and food security — India has now emerged as a decisive player.

AMERICAN OVERVIEW: ASIAN POLICY CHALLENGES FOR THE NEXT PRESIDENT

Michael H. Armacost and J. Stapleton Roy

In a few short months, a new U.S. administration will take office in Washington. It will inherit a decent hand to play in Asia. The region is not currently in crisis. Relations among the great powers there – the United States, Japan, China, Russia, and India – are generally constructive. The prospect of conflict among them is remote. Asian economies have sustained robust growth despite the current U.S. slowdown. The results of recent elections in both South Korea and Taiwan present promising opportunities that did not exist a year ago. Counter-terrorist efforts in Southeast Asia have produced some impressive results. The North Korean nuclear issue is belatedly getting front burner attention. And the image of the United States has been selectively enhanced by its generous response to natural disasters in the region.

Despite this, the region needs urgent attention. In contrast to Europe, where EU integration has submerged the centuries-old destructive rivalries that spawned two world wars; in Asia, the nation-state system remains strong, balance of power considerations dominate thinking in most of the region's capitals, and America's relative power has been declining.

Accommodating the rise of newly emerging great powers without conflict is always a daunting challenge. Yet in Asia we face not the rise of a single new power, but several. China will present the most formidable geopolitical challenge, but India is also looking for a "place in the sun." And the greater assertiveness we can expect from Japan, Russia, and other Asian countries is merely part of a larger phenomenon that Fareed Zakaria has appropriately dubbed "the rise of the rest."

While the United States has been preoccupied with the situation in the Middle East, the Asian balance has been shifting quietly, if inexorably, in the direction of others. China, Japan, India, and Russia are casting a longer shadow. Size matters, and they have it. In 2007 China contributed more to global growth than America did – the first time this has occurred since the 1930s. India's economy is growing almost as fast as China's, and it is becoming an important source of entrepreneurial innovation. Russia's power is expanding in pace with the rising price of energy resources, and Moscow is determined to exploit its new situation not only for commercial advantage but strategic leverage as well. Although Japanese growth proceeds at a more stately pace, its economy is three times the size of China's, and dwarfs India's and Russia's. Tokyo, moreover, continues steadily to amend the self-imposed restrictions that have, for decades, limited its international security role, as it seeks to become a "more normal nation."

What then should be the key features of a plausible U.S. strategy toward Asia? The starting point must be a willingness to accord Asia the attention its intrinsic importance to us demands. After all, Asia contains over half the world's population, and six of its ten largest countries. It produces more than 30 percent of global exports, and controls a much larger share of the world's savings pool. It is in Asia that the interests of the Great Powers intersect most directly, and the most consequential emerging powers — China and India — are located. Iran may pose the most dangerous threat of nuclear proliferation, but North Korea presents the more urgent challenge since it has already tested a nuclear "device." Asia also contains the three countries – Indonesia, Pakistan, and India – with the largest Muslim populations. Asia is also the most dynamic region in the world economy. It is there that we run our largest and most persistent deficits and where we tap the gigantic Asian savings pools to finance our trade deficits and offset our puny national savings rate. These are ample reasons to pay more attention to Asia and to give our policies in the region a higher priority in the next administration.

What then should be the key features of a plausible U.S. strategy toward Asia? The starting point must be a willingness to accord Asia the attention its intrinsic importance to us demands. After all, Asia contains over half the world's population, and six of its ten largest countries. It produces more than 30 percent of global exports, and controls a much larger share of the world's savings pool.

The first task for the next administration must be the articulation of a serviceable set of goals for intensified American policy efforts in the Asian region. It cannot depend on the post-September 11 U.S. National Security Strategy that placed reliance upon the preventive use of force and the promotion of regime change. This approach was heavily discredited by our experience in Iraq.

Our choices are limited. We cannot downgrade relations with Asia or retreat from major responsibilities in the region at a time when its importance to U.S. interests is growing. Nor can we place our faith in collective security arrangements; there is no broadly shared perception of threat, and many disputes over borders persist. Willy-nilly, we must continue to perform the duties of an off-shore balancer, and that role is more readily acquitted with our current allies than without them.

The first task for the next administration must be the articulation of a serviceable set of goals for intensified American policy efforts in the Asian region. It cannot depend on the post-September 11 U.S. National Security Strategy that placed reliance upon the preventive use of force and the promotion of regime change. This approach was heavily discredited by our experience in Iraq.

The growing strength of other potential Asian great powers imposes several new requirements on American policy.

1. Our policy toward Asia starts at home. We need to augment the underpinnings of American competitiveness across the board, and we need to focus on the long haul. Our population is aging; "baby boomers" are on the threshold of retirement; our entitlement programs are urgently in need of reform; our rate of productivity growth has slackened; the cost of oil and

other resources has skyrocketed; our national savings rate has plummeted; immigration of skilled labor has slowed; foreign direct investment in the United States has tapered off even as the dollar has weakened. Post-September 11 security measures have saddled us with higher overhead costs and lower efficiency. Our K-12 educational system is spotty, and our politicians appear increasingly reluctant to defend the principles of free trade. These are all troubling straws in the wind. Unless corrected, the U.S. economy will be unable to outperform other rich countries as we have for the past decade and a half. Almost all structural remedies of consequence will require bipartisanship at a time when it appears in short supply.

Our policy toward Asia starts at home. We need to augment the underpinnings of American competitiveness across the board, and we need to focus on the long haul.

---

2. We need to refine our strategic doctrine. As outlined by the current administration, the United States has sought unchallengeable international supremacy. A declared objective is to dissuade others from becoming "peer competitors." If we retain this goal, then China's rise, or for that matter the rise of any other major Asian power, will be seen at some point as a threat to the United States, regardless of that country's conduct. Sooner or later a "containment" effort will be required. If, on the other hand, the United States defines its goal more modestly as ensuring the security and prosperity of the American people, America need not feel threatened by stronger or more pros-

perous Asian powers, so long as they behave responsibly.
The goal then can be to encourage moderate external conduct
through the cultivation of balanced ties with all the emerging
powers. Indeed the operational rule for policy should be to
maintain better ties with each of the other major powers than
they can forge between themselves. Such an approach can maximize American leverage while minimizing threats to our security
and prosperity.

Indeed the operational rule for policy should be to maintain bet-

ter ties with each of the other major powers than they can forge

between themselves. Such an approach can maximize American

leverage while minimizing threats to our security and prosperity.

---

3. We face in Asia a host of transnational challenges that demand
   redress. They include the dangers of nuclear proliferation, the
   persistent threat from Islamic jihadis, the need for enhanced
   energy security, the growing risks of global warming, the uncertainties of public health pandemics, and the recent failures of
   multilateral efforts to liberalize global trade. If we do not take
   the lead in stimulating regional and global initiatives to tackle
   these problems, who will? When the cold war ended, our primacy increased. Yet, others did not forge a counter-coalition as
   a hedge against our dominance. In part this was because
   America continued to shoulder a disproportionate share of the
   cost of public goods. We extended protection to many weak
   nations; we espoused the principles of free trade; we supported

the development of institutions that constrained on occasion our own freedom of diplomatic maneuverability. Unfortunately, we have been investing less in such public goods that demonstrate to others the continuing value of our friendship.

We face then a triple challenge: getting our own house in order, defining with greater clarity a geopolitical strategy for Asia, and promoting concerted efforts among Asian powers to cope with pressing transnational problems.

We face then a triple challenge: getting our own house in order,

defining with greater clarity a geopolitical strategy for Asia, and

promoting concerted efforts among Asian powers to cope with

pressing transnational problems.

The distractions will be many. However large the challenges of Asia may loom, the new administration must also cope with a weakened dollar, inconclusive wars in Iraq and Afghanistan, a persistent terrorist threat from al-Qaeda, growing concerns about global warming, and looming problems at home — including healthcare costs, social security reform, infrastructure degradation, and a sluggish economy. These issues can be expected initially to demand the lion's share of the new administration's attention.

Even with the best of intentions, the new administration will be hard-pressed in its initial months to address the array of issues demanding attention. The United States is the only major country that sweeps away the entire policymaking echelon of the government every time the White House changes hands. It will take time for the new administration to put its ducks into a row; i.e. to pick a new foreign policy team, secure their confirmation from the Senate, sort out new policy priorities, and establish working relationships with the Congress and the press.

These factors will limit the amount of serious and sustained attention that the new U.S. administration is likely initially to devote to the situation in Asia. But it cannot afford to put Asia on the back burner.

Regional Trends

In essence, there are two separate but complementary tendencies discernable in the current dynamics of change in East Asia:

- The first is the inclination on the part of Asian nations to balance and dilute China's growing influence by embedding it into a web of relationships that subtly constrain Beijing's freedom to maneuver.

- The second is a comparable desire to limit and balance the role of the United States, reflecting a widely felt discomfort with a unipolar world, the assertive style of recent U.S. leadership, and our perceived propensity to act unilaterally without adequate regard to how our actions affect the interests of others.

Both tendencies are at work in the impulse to create new regional institutional arrangements. For the moment, these tendencies are not aimed at containing China or excluding the United States from Asia. On the contrary, there is a near universal desire to engage China constructively and to continue working with the

United States on regional problems. These dynamics are largely positive, but it is far from clear whether Asia's institution-building efforts will be sufficient to manage great power rivalries and ensure the continuation of a peaceful and stable East Asian environment in the absence of more active and purposeful American involvement.

Another fundamental aspect of contemporary East Asia is the absence of any consensus on the role the United States should play in a nascent regional community. In part, this merely reflects the extraordinary geographical diversity of the arc that sweeps from Northeast Asia through Southeast Asia to Afghanistan and Pakistan in the west. Despite the bridging function provided by the 10 countries of the Association of Southeast Asian Nations (ASEAN), East Asia and South Asia retain largely separate identities. This is changing, driven in large measure by complex and evolving patterns of cooperation and rivalry between China and India – indeed, for that matter between all the emerging powers in Asia that are seeking to expand their influence throughout the region.

Meanwhile, the United States has been steadily adapting its security footprint in Asia. This has entailed troop reductions in South Korea, adjustment of basing arrangements in Japan, increasing reliance on Guam as a power-projection platform, changing ad hoc patterns of defense cooperation in Southeast Asia, and the evolution of a more robust strategic partnership with India. Some elements of this approach have the flavor of an incipient containment strategy against China — such as Washington's recent emphasis on "values-based diplomacy," its quest for a League of Asian Democracies, and proposals for quadripartite meetings of the United States, Japan, Australia, and India. For now, however, a containment strategy aimed at Beijing would be at best premature, and at worst, counterproductive.

These changes in American security policy have been driven more by shifts in U.S. strategic concepts than by consultations with regional allies. As a result, there is a discernible undercurrent of uneasiness about the strength of the U.S. commitment to regional security and its future trajectory.

Meanwhile, the center of gravity in regional community building has continued to shift from trans-Pacific to pan-Asian venues. This trend gained additional momentum with the holding of the first East Asia Summit in Kuala Lumpur in December 2005 and the ensuing decision to make these summits annual events. Even though these meetings included all the major players in East Asia, Washington foreswore participation. While China, Japan, India, Russia, and Australia all acceded to the ASEAN Treaty of Amity and Cooperation — a requirement for membership in the East Asia Summit — the United States remained a holdout. At the same time, China has energetically and successfully pursued closer ties with the ASEAN region; and Japan and India, among others, have actively followed suit.

On the economic front, intra-regional trade has expanded enormously, as have investment flows and technology transfers. Intra-Asian economic integration is now proceeding more rapidly than trans-Pacific exchanges of goods, services, and capital. It is noteworthy that by 2006 China replaced the United States as the number one trading partner of Japan, South Korea, and Taiwan, as well as most Southeast Asian countries. As Asian countries have accelerated their growth, their skyrocketing demand for energy and other resources has pushed up prices for scarce commodities; while intensifying environmental challenges related to water, forests, and, of course, the earth's atmosphere.

Key Alliances

Against this background, the new U.S. administration will confront further pressures for policy adjustments. It will need to take a comprehensive look at the security architecture in Asia. Our defense relationships in Asia are largely an inheritance from the Cold War. Key partnerships with Japan, South Korea, and Australia continue to serve us well. Nevertheless, conditions have changed, and a review would be desirable to determine how well these legacy arrangements suit the circumstances we are likely to face over the coming decades in Asia.

Our defense relationships in Asia are largely an inheritance from the Cold War. Key partnerships with Japan, South Korea, and Australia continue to serve us well. Nevertheless, conditions have changed, and a review would be desirable to determine how well these legacy arrangements suit the circumstances we are likely to face over the coming decades in Asia.

- **The U.S.-Japan alliance** has become more balanced, more global, and more operational in recent years – a welcome evolution from the standpoint of American interests. But there has also been some recent drift – not least because of the paralysis in Japanese politics. With one party controlling the Lower House and another in charge in the Upper House, much legislation

has reached an impasse. Progress on base issues – e.g., the
movement of U.S. Marines from Futenma – has stalled. The
conduct of U.S. diplomacy toward North Korea has inspired
Japanese misgivings regarding the quality of consultations,
and even provoked some charges of "betrayal." Pyongyang's test
of a nuclear device in 2006 prompted some Japanese officials to
wonder about the future efficacy of "extended deterrence," and
to contemplate changes in their longstanding "non-nuclear
principles." And Washington's refusal to authorize sale of the F-
22 fighter aircraft rankles. In the aggregate, these developments
have produced Japanese frustration, malaise, and a heightened
sense of isolation. The new administration will have to find
ways of drawing Tokyo more actively into trilateral consultations
with Seoul and Washington prior to Six-Party Talks meetings.
It should push for trilateral meetings on security and other
issues with Japan and China. And without dwelling on the "UK
of Asia" model, it should leave no doubt about the priority we
accord to the U.S.-Japan alliance as the hub of our Asian security
policy, and our willingness to take practical steps to bolster the
credibility of our nuclear umbrella.

- **In South Korea** the recent presidential and legislative elections
  have produced a more conservative ROK administration that is
  well disposed to the U.S. alliance, determined to engage the
  North on a more reciprocal basis, and prepared to expand economic collaboration with Pyongyang — but only as the North
  proceeds to dismantle its nuclear capabilities. This should permit closer coordination of U.S., ROK, and Japanese negotiating
  tactics for dealing with Pyongyang in the Six-Party Talks. As
  President Lee Myung-bak has affirmed his interest in defining a
  wider role in the world, there is also an opportunity to develop
  a broader regional and global diplomatic partnership with the
  ROK. At the same time, the domestic political backlash against

President Lee for allegedly being too deferential to the United States on the beef import issue illustrates the care that must be taken in managing this critically important relationship. In particular, U.S. policy toward North Korea must take into account the views of our South Korean ally.

• **Australia** is a trusted friend that can be counted on when the chips are down. It values the U.S. relationship above all others, but its prosperity and security are inextricably linked to the quality of its ties with Asia. The United States can only benefit from paying close attention to Australian views and keeping the alliance robust.

The North Korean Nuclear Issue

As for North Korea, putting a cap back on its plutonium program is a worthy accomplishment, even if the program is capped at a higher level than in 2002. "Denuclearization" will have to be pursued by the next administration. It will not be easy. North Korean authorities may not have relinquished their hopes that in time other countries will grudgingly acquiesce in their status as a nuclear power. Certainly their diplomacy has raised the tactics of "buying time" and exploiting the differences among their interlocutors into a fine art.

It will be important that the next administration not get off on the wrong foot on this issue, as the current administration did in 2001. In particular, a prolonged hiatus in the talks that provides the occasion for Pyongyang to conduct a second nuclear weapons test or resume long-range missile tests would precipitate a crisis and have unpredictable consequences. The new administration must also be prepared for the possibility that the talks could fail. In such a situation, it will be important that Seoul, Beijing, and Tokyo attribute a breakdown to North Korean obduracy. If they blame U.S. inflexibility for the breakdown, we can forget about any possibility of applying tougher sanctions on Pyongyang.

Managing Relations with China

U.S. relations with China depend not simply on how we define our broad foreign policy goals, but on how we handle a host of China-related issues. Among these, economic issues are likely to be front and center. The administration has effectively utilized the talents of senior officials in State and Treasury to strengthen bilateral dialogue mechanisms with Beijing that have improved policy coordination and helped forestall ill-advised Congressional initiatives on trade and currency issues. These dialogues should be sustained by a new administration.

China's military modernization programs require special attention. The new administration will need to distinguish between (1) generic PLA modernization that will undoubtedly continue in pace with the expansion of China's economy, and (2) potentially destabilizing programs aimed at rapid acquisition of capabilities specifically targeted against Taiwan that could complicate threat calculations and raise doubts about Beijing's intentions. The first requires prudent attention. The second should be addressed through a strategy aimed at lowering tension in the Taiwan Strait. Public rhetoric about China's military capabilities also needs to be coherent and calibrated to avoid extremes of complacency or reckless ringing of alarm bells. Common sense would suggest that the United States should not presume to define China's defense needs for it.

Given the sensitivity of the Taiwan issue in U.S.-China relations, the new administration needs to move promptly to reaffirm our position on Taiwan and to determine its approach to managing our important unofficial relationship with Taiwan.

- **Cross-Strait relations.** For a number of reasons, the firmness of the current administration's position on Taiwan has helped to stabilize the cross-Strait relationship during a period of acute mistrust between Beijing and Taipei. The recent Taiwan elections have opened up prospects for an expansion of cross-Strait contacts and a lowering of tensions. It is still too early to tell how this will affect the situation six months from now. The question is whether Beijing and Taipei will display the statesmanship necessary to translate this promising opening into a durable stabilization of the cross-Strait relationship. Initial indicators are positive. U.S. policymakers must weigh how best to facilitate this process.

- **Arms sales to Taiwan.** A key challenge for U.S. policymakers will be how to calibrate arms sales to Taiwan to a lowered threat posture in the strait area if the People's Republic of China makes some confidence-building moves. These might, for example, include halting exercises in the strait area and/or redeploying some missiles. If the PRC makes such positive moves and we do not show any reflection of this in our own policy, then a promising opportunity to work back toward a lowered threat posture in the strait will have been lost. We cannot make such moves through prior agreement with the PRC since the Taiwan Relations Act must drive our arms sales (not the arms makers); but if the threat is lessened, we will have a basis for appropriate responses.

• Managing unofficial relations with Taiwan. Our unofficial relationship with Taiwan is both unique and fraught with sensitivi-
ties. In international affairs, it is rare that one can eat one's cake
and have it too. Hence, we should assume that there will be
tough trade-offs between trying to increase the officiality of our
links with Taiwan and gaining more international space for the
island. We think the U.S. interest is better served by putting the
focus on expanding Taiwan's international running room. That
must be done, to be sure, within the confines of a restored 1992
consensus under which Taiwan does not constantly test the constraints in areas that do not involve fundamental sovereignty
issues, e.g., UN membership. However, this is a policy question
that needs the careful attention of the new administration.

Southeast Asia

In Southeast Asia, the new administration should consider ways to
derive greater benefit from our relationship with ASEAN. Our
ability to work with ASEAN collectively has been constrained by
Washington's reluctance to have Burma (also known as Myanmar)
at the table. Burma remains an "outlier," and neither our reliance
on sanctions nor ASEAN's preference for a softer approach has
produced noteworthy results. Under these circumstances, this issue
needs a new look. ASEAN cohesion is an important factor in containing bilateral frictions in Southeast Asia, in enhancing the
region's ability to deal more effectively with the rising colossus of
China, and in retaining a lead role in building a wider Asian community. Washington now needs to find a way to work collectively
with ASEAN in ways that would strengthen the organization.
There is an important congressional aspect to this, but that should
not be an excuse for failing to look for a more effective policy.

South Asia

In South Asia, there has been substantial improvement in U.S. bilateral relations with India. Clearly the U.S.-India Nuclear Agreement was a keystone of that advance, and if it has not been ratified, the new administration must make an early determination whether it is sustainable. Convergent interests in the fields of security, economics, and educational exchange provide ample scope for expanding bilateral cooperation. And, happily, India-Pakistan tensions have eased. Shared concerns about energy security and environmental degradation may best be tackled in multilateral venues. The larger point is that one of the most positive legacies a new administration will inherit will be the opportunity to cooperate with India, as Henry Kissinger has noted, "on both ideological and strategic grounds."

Our ability to work with ASEAN collectively has been constrained by Washington's reluctance to have Burma (also known as Myanmar) at the table. Burma remains an "outlier," and neither our reliance on sanctions nor ASEAN's preference for a softer approach has produced noteworthy results. Under these circumstances, this issue needs a new look.

The picture in Pakistan is less promising. Its political stability is fragile. The military retains its dominance; civilian institutions have not flourished. The Taliban has been resuscitated. The Northwest Frontier provinces have become a safe haven for terrorists, increasing incentives for cross-border preemptive strikes. How to bolster the Pakistani military's effectiveness in bringing order to these remote areas without pushing them into an expanded political role; how to overcome domestic resistance to the provision of wider market access in the United States for Pakistani textiles; and how subtly to help the civilian government of Pakistan to weather the inevitable strains to which it is subject will be among the key challenges for a new administration.

And in Afghanistan, security conditions have deteriorated at a time when North Atlantic Treaty Organization (NATO) countries are reluctant to volunteer additional forces. The drug trade provides expanding financial support for the insurgency, and the corruption of local officials makes it difficult to gain headway against it. A new administration will have to devote more effort and resources to combating the drug trade by helping to cultivate alternative crops and working with the Government of Afghanistan to find an effective eradication method for poppies.

Transnational Policy Challenges

In order to tackle a host of pressing transnational challenges and take some of the sharp edges off of geopolitical maneuvering among Asian powers, the next administration should explore possibilities for augmenting collaboration with all major Asian powers.

Nuclear Proliferation. The viability of the Non-Proliferation Treaty (NPT) regime has been eroded by the nuclear activities of North Korea and Iran. The U.S.-India Nuclear Agreement has also reinforced a perception that the United States attaches diminished importance to that regime. The next administration must take steps to ameliorate that perception. As four prominent American statesmen – George Shultz, Henry Kissinger, Bill Perry, and Sam Nunn – have recently written, "We face a very real possibility that the deadliest weapons ever invented could fall into dangerous hands. The steps we are taking now to address these threats are not adequate to the danger."

We will have no possibility of persuading others to forego their nuclear ambitions if we are unprepared to put more serious effort into reducing our own arsenal and modernizing the NPT. And this will require visible changes in our nuclear policy. Whether the vision of a "zero nuclear world" is realistically attainable remains highly uncertain. But there are a host of steps – e.g., major reductions in our own nuclear arsenal, augmented efforts to enhance the safety and security of currently deployed weapons, some internationalization of the nuclear fuel cycle, a ratification of the Comprehensive Test Ban Treaty, etc. – which are worthy of exploration.

We will have no possibility of persuading others to forego their

nuclear ambitions if we are unprepared to put more serious effort

into reducing our own arsenal and modernizing the NPT.

And this will require visible changes in our nuclear policy.

In the first instance, we would need to enlist the cooperation of the Russians. If we can make headway with Moscow, this might give impetus to a broader effort to modernize the NPT. The cooperation of Japan, India, China, and others would be essential. It is unclear, and unlikely, that the two-tiered NPT system can be sustained. What is obvious is that if wholesale increases in the number of nuclear weapons states is to be avoided, we will have to provide the lead, and elicit the cooperation of other key countries who either possess such weapons or aspire to their acquisition.

Countering Terrorism. The Global War on Terror was an unfortunate misnomer. It encouraged excessive emphasis on military force. It conflated a host of differing political forces whose interests often diverged. It persuaded some that the enemy was Islam, rather than a few misguided groups within Islam's ranks disposed to a permanent jihad against the "infidels." We should not lump potential Islamist enemies together; the trick is to divide them, and deal with them in a discriminating way. And we should take account of successes and learn from the methods that produced them.

The Global War on Terror was an unfortunate misnomer. It encouraged excessive emphasis on military force. It conflated a host of differing political forces whose interests often diverged. It persuaded some that the enemy was Islam, rather than a few misguided groups within Islam's ranks disposed to a permanent jihad against the "infidels."

In Southeast Asia, intelligence sharing, cooperative police work, and coordinated efforts to deprive al-Qaeda and local affiliates of their traditional sources of financing have produced surprisingly impressive results. These were doubtless facilitated by a growing awareness that most victims of terrorist attacks were local Muslims. This has outraged many Muslim leaders and prompted some to speak out against co-religionists who use the Koran to justify unspeakable violence against innocent civilians.

The picture is less encouraging in South Asia, and especially in Pakistan — where the remnants of the Taliban have regrouped; where safe havens for terrorist training exist in the Northwest tribal areas; and where cross-border assaults against known terrorists in, for example, Waziristan are now provoking violent responses against soft targets in Pakistani urban areas, thereby fueling additional political turmoil.

Meanwhile, in Afghanistan, the local insurgency continues to fester, as noted above. The next administration will have its hands full in South Asia.

The next administration will have its hands full in South Asia.

Energy Cooperation. The high cost of energy is becoming a major threat to the continued growth and prosperity of Asia, just as it is elsewhere in the world. Ensuring access to energy resources is a top foreign policy priority of states throughout the region. Meanwhile, producer nations appear intent on keeping energy prices at unusually high levels. We consequently face a massive crunch on resources.

The United States can make a major contribution to containing these incentives for rivalry by encouraging policies that foster cooperative approaches to energy security. Most Asian countries are major consumers of imported fuels. All would benefit from expanded cooperation with the United States in efforts to persuade the Organization of the Petroleum Exporting Countries (OPEC) and other producers to expand exploration for oil and natural gas, to accelerate the commercial development of alternative environmentally friendly fuels, to utilize existing sources of energy more efficiently, and to stockpile reserves for emergencies. In this connection, the requirement that membership in the International Energy Agency remain based on participation in the Organization for Economic Cooperation and Development (OECD) makes little sense. It excludes the two-largest contemporary sources of new energy demand – China and India. The next administration should break this nexus, and open the door to membership to the major energy consuming nations of Asia.

The health of the U.S. economy is now tied to Asia in fundamental ways that if not grasped quickly by the new administration could have unintended and potentially adverse consequences.

International Economic Cooperation. The health of the U.S. economy is now tied to Asia in fundamental ways that if not grasped quickly by the new administration could have unintended and potentially adverse consequences. Asian countries hold roughly half of the world's foreign currency reserves – some $3 trillion – which gives them formidable financial leverage; arguably even the possibility of going their own way if, in their judgment, global financial institutions are unresponsive to their interests and fail to acknowledge their growing heft in the world economy. Already Asians are creating regional bank swap arrangements and promoting a regional bond market. They are proliferating bilateral and regional free trade agreements. They are fashioning national sovereign wealth funds to invest in assets that offer higher returns than U.S. Treasuries. These linkages will become clearer as the current global financial crisis runs its course and demonstrates whether flagging U.S. economic performance will significantly slow Asian economies or, conversely, whether their continued buoyancy will help pull the U.S. economy out of a slump.

Regardless, a number of trade-related issues will need to be high on the agenda of the new administration: namely, the restoration of fast-track negotiating authority, the completion of the Doha round, the ratification of the US-ROK Free Trade Agreement, and determination of the weight to be attached to Asia-Pacific Economic Cooperation (APEC) in pursuing Asian trade initiatives. Neglect of these issues will deal a body blow to U.S. global economic leadership.

Regardless, a number of trade-related issues will need to be high on the agenda of the new administration: namely, the restoration of fast-track negotiating authority, the completion of the Doha round, the ratification of the US-ROK Free Trade Agreement, and determination of the weight to be attached to Asia-Pacific Economic Cooperation (APEC) in pursuing Asian trade initiatives. Neglect of these issues will deal a body blow to U.S. global economic leadership.

Cooperation to Clean Up the Environment. The Asian region faces the world's most severe environmental challenges as economic growth has outpaced the adoption of measures to ensure supplies of clean air and water. U.S. leadership in this area has lagged as we have questioned the scientific case for global warming and rejected the Kyoto protocols without offering credible alternatives. The consequences are becoming more immediate as Asian pollution is beginning adversely to affect the environment in parts of the United States. U.S. self-interest alone should place the necessity for a more active approach on this issue high on the agenda of the new administration. A central requirement will be a policy approach that is not perceived by the major developing states of Asia as a constraint on their future growth prospects. China and India are heavily reliant on coal to meet their power needs. If they face a choice between assuming expanded environmental responsibilities and accepting slower growth, or sustaining high gross national product (GNP) growth at the cost of polluting the planet, they will opt for the latter. Kyoto-style limits have been a non-starter with them, certainly in the absence of a fund provided by wealthy countries to cover the incremental costs of greener but more expensive power plants. Assistance in the transfer of key technologies will be essential. One example of the kinds of projects that would pay dividends would be collaboration with India and China, among others, to test coal gasification with carbon capture and sequestration on a commercial scale.

A central requirement will be a policy approach that is not perceived by the major developing states of Asia as a constraint on their future growth prospects.

Regional Community Building. As a priority matter, the new administration will also need to define more clearly how the United States intends to position itself with respect to the East Asia community-building process. Do we wish to be an "inside" or an "outside" player, and what balance should be struck between these alternative approaches? The United States has been only modestly engaged in the East Asia community-building process, and has largely adopted a "wait and see" posture. We have put scant thought or energy into APEC, while remaining aloof from the ASEAN Plus Three and the East Asian Summit.

This relatively passive posture is scarcely commensurate with the degree to which U.S. interests may be affected by new institutional arrangements. It also means that U.S. engagement in the intellectual process of thinking through these issues is lagging behind that of Asians, who have been intensely focused on community building for much of the last decade. East Asians have not yet formed definitive ideas about the organizational structures that are best suited to managing emerging regional realities. It is precisely for this reason that deeper U.S. involvement is so important. Key Asian countries currently find themselves in an awkward position. They are taking steps to which the United States will eventually react, though for the moment the United States is merely watching from the sidelines. We have, to be sure, promoted one sub-regional effort – the Six-Party Talks – to tackle the North Korean nuclear problem. If further headway is achieved, this could serve as the embryo for broader security collaboration in Northeast Asia – an area bereft of institutional arrangements to ameliorate regional rivalries.

Global Governance. It is already apparent that existing global institutions are not configured in ways that accurately reflect contemporary power realities. The UN Security Council under-represents the emerging powers and excludes major global players such as Japan from a permanent seat; The World Bank and International Monetary Fund (IMF) pursue purposes that have not been adequately redefined to meet current needs. The G-8 extends membership to Canada, but not China; to Italy, but not India; to Russia, but not Brazil. The group's deficiencies should be remedied. To better accommodate Asia's rising power, China and India should be included. Reforming the United Nations, the World Bank, and IMF pose tougher dilemmas because of their wider membership. Progress will doubtless be slow. But the new administration should put these matters on the agenda, and devote high-level attention to them.

Democracy and Human Rights. The new administration would be well advised to modulate its rhetoric on promoting democracy and human rights. This does not mean downgrading or downplaying the importance of these issues. Economic development has been the principal driver of democratic change in East Asia. Respect for human rights has increased as governing systems have become more representative. Yet neither economic development nor the introduction of more pluralistic politics can be accomplished overnight. These processes generally take decades. The United States can promote respect for democracy and human rights most effectively by providing an example for others to emulate — by keeping our doors open to Asians who seek access to U.S. colleges and universities; by strengthening our International Military Education and Training (IMET) programs; by encouraging the work of non-governmental organizations fostering judicial and political reform; and by lending our political and moral weight to wider respect for openness, diversity, and pluralism throughout Asia.

We have, then, identified a host of policy challenges and opportunities for the new administration. They include:

- Devoting to Asian issues the attention and resources their intrinsic importance to the United States demands.

- Maintaining a favorable Asian balance in the face of rapidly rising Chinese and Indian power, determined Japanese and Russian efforts to expand their clout, and perceptions that the U.S. role is diminishing.

- Putting our approach to counter-terrorism in the Middle East and South Asia on a new strategic footing that neither overshadows nor underrates a host of other foreign policy challenges.

- Clarifying the American role in fashioning a regional community in Asia from which we have remained relatively aloof.

- Preserving a cohesive U.S.-Japanese alliance at a moment when more Japanese are asking tough questions about the reliability of our "extended deterrence."

- Retaining a constructive response to China's relentless "rise."

- Capitalizing on recent election outcomes in South Korea and Taiwan to bolster the U.S.-ROK alliance and ease cross-Strait tensions.

- Adjusting our approaches to the changing political dynamics in Southeast Asia and South Asia.

- Curbing the spread of nuclear weapons at a time when the continued viability of the two-tiered NPT is under stress.

- According a higher priority to energy security and environmental issues in Asia and beyond.

- Responding to the "rise of the rest" by adjusting the membership in various international organizations.

These and other issues are addressed in greater detail in the series of policy briefs commissioned by The Asia Foundation, and included in this volume. We hope that policy advisers to the Democratic and Republican presidential candidates will read them carefully and heed their thoughtful advice.

U.S. ECONOMIC POLICY TOWARD ASIA FOR THE INCOMING ADMINISTRATION

Marcus Noland

Issue: A new U.S. administration will be under pressure to quickly determine its position on a host of trade, investment, and financial issues, including: a) bilateral and/or multilateral free trade agreements as policy instruments; b) the completion of the Doha Development Round; c) exchange rate questions, including the weakening U.S. dollar; and d) trade imbalances. Is there a coherent integrated strategy that can address these multiple issues? Can these issues be addressed simultaneously, and, if not, how should they be prioritized? Can remedial solutions be found without undertaking corresponding domestic economic and financial measures?

Introduction

Economically, Asia is a region of considerable diversity: some of its economies include major international investors and technological innovators, while others continue to employ large parts of their workforces in agriculture and receive concessional assistance from the international community. For the most part, the U.S. policy agenda toward Asia does not revolve around regional issues. Instead, U.S. economic policy toward Asia is largely derived from its global economic policies. From the standpoint of Asian governments, the issues of greatest salience in their relationship with the United States are either bilateral in nature, or are the bilateral manifestation of issues of global concern.

With that said, increasing intra-regional trade and investment are forging a stronger Asian regional identity than existed in the past. This creates some paradoxical challenges for American policymakers. Regional diversity militates against defining U.S. policy in regional terms, and the national interests of Asian countries diverge on many policy issues – yet the emergence in Asia of regional institutions and initiatives requires a U.S. response. The United States will host the Asia Pacific Economic Cooperation (APEC) forum in 2011, forcing Asian regional issues onto the agenda of the next administration.

The United States will host the Asia Pacific Economic Cooperation (APEC) forum in 2011, forcing Asian regional issues onto the agenda of the next administration.

Unlike many of the more traditional diplomatic issues discussed in other contributions to this volume, where the administration acts with relative autonomy, U.S. economic diplomacy is significantly affected by both market developments and U.S. domestic politics. The incoming administration will face two specific challenges in organizing American economic diplomacy toward Asia. First, there is a risk that the financial market turmoil will have a substantial negative impact on both the United States and global economy. Second, there is a domestic political environment that makes it increasingly difficult to formulate a constructive trade policy. Some of the critical items on the U.S. economic agenda with Asia — establishing a viable policy on sovereign wealth funds, the Korea-U.S. Free Trade Agreement (KORUS), and the Doha Development

Round of multilateral trade negotiations under the auspices of the World Trade Organization, to name three — may require immediate attention, and may or may not be specifically "Asian" per se.

Macroeconomic and Financial Context

The next administration will likely have to confront the largest global financial crisis since the Asian crisis of 1997-98. Estimated losses among banks, insurance firms, and other institutions currently approximate $1 trillion. This episode could amount to a watershed event. Depending on the specifics of the unfolding crisis and the outcome of the November 2008 elections, the United States could reverse the trend toward financial market deregulation begun during the Carter administration. A key question is whether such reregulation would adversely affect U.S. economic performance, possibly contributing to a decline in the relative importance of the United States in the global economy and reducing American diplomatic relevance.

The next administration will likely have to confront the largest global financial crisis since the Asian crisis of 1997-98. Estimated losses among banks, insurance firms, and other institutions currently approximate $1 trillion.

Reregulation would also change the ideological context of international policy formation. Less pressure on Asian countries for financial market liberalization would emanate from multilateral organizations such as the International Monetary Fund (IMF), World Bank, and Asian Development Bank (ADB). Such a lag would presumably be reflected in the U.S. trade negotiation agenda — with less confidence in unfettered financial market operation, and U.S. policy swinging back toward regulation, U.S. demands for Asian countries to liberalize their financial markets and grant U.S. service providers greater access would eventually attenuate or become less effective.

Heightened interest in the regulation of sovereign wealth funds (SWFs) will be of immediate relevance to Asian sovereign investors. The IMF is facilitating a dialogue on identifying best practices for SWFs and the Organisation for Economic Co-operation and Development (OECD) is running a counterpart operation for SWF investment recipient countries. In March, the United States, United Arab Emirates, and Singapore — home to some of the oldest SWFs — announced a code of conduct, which they hope will gain adherents and form the basis for a global standard.

Some Asian countries have benefitted substantially from the rapid growth of consumption in the United States since 1994, and there has been some talk of "de-coupling": the hope that rapid growth elsewhere, particularly in China, might cushion the blow as the U.S. economy slows or enters recession. However, rather than "de-coupling," Asia may well experience "reverse coupling," as a combination of slowdown in the United States and depreciation of the U.S. dollar leads to a substantial, sustained increase in U.S. net exports.

The bilateral trade imbalance with China ballooned to $252 billion in 2007, accounting for more than one-third of America's global trade deficit of over $700 billion. China's exchange rate policy will also be a source of ongoing concern. In the long run, China will experience significant real appreciation generated by its rising productivity in its traded goods sector, and exchange rate policy will move toward a more genuine float. But getting to this outcome will be politically contentious, and the next administration will face congressional pressure on the Chinese currency issue.

Regional Macroeconomic Cooperation

In the decade since the 1997-98 crisis, Asian disappointment with Washington writ large has encouraged a push for both greater influence in global institutions such as the IMF, as well as more robust regional institutions and arrangements.

At the IMF, quota allocations (in principle reflecting the importance of individual countries in the world economy) determine the amount of foreign exchange countries make available for IMF use, board representation, and notionally the level of IMF borrowing for which a member is eligible. Asia remains underweighted despite recent quota reallocations. More radical recalibrations have been blocked by Western Europe, which is over-weighted. The United States, with a quota share of 17 percent, has allowed its own quota to decline (though not enough to imperil its sole veto power over Executive Board decisions under the 85 percent qualified majority voting system). To satisfy Asian desires, it might be possible to combine Western Europe into a single European Union, or Eurozone, quota and reallocate to Asia and other underrepresented areas the remaining freed quota. Yet to accomplish this, Western European governments would have to be willing to sacrifice national prerogatives, and the United States might have to surrender its veto monopoly. Thus far, European intransigence has allowed the United States to duck this conundrum. As for Asia, there is no single dominant economy equivalent to the United

States, nor the degree of formal regional integration like the European Union or Eurozone, which could make accumulation into a single regional voice possible.

As for Asia, there is no single dominant economy equivalent to the United States, nor the degree of formal regional integration like the European Union or Eurozone, which could make accumulation into a single regional voice possible.

Instead, the Asians have increasingly focused on regional initiatives. In the financial sphere the most prominent of these initiatives has been the Chiang Mai Initiative (CMI), a three-part cooperation framework instituting a network of bilateral medium-term foreign exchange credit arrangements among the central banks; undertaking regional macroeconomic surveillance; and committing to technical assistance. Sixteen bilateral swap agreements amounting to as much as US$83 billion have been concluded, with further growth expected. The Asians are also pursuing other regional initiatives, such as the promotion of a regional bond market and the adoption of a common basket currency peg, with the Japanese-led ADB effectively serving as the secretariat.

To some observers, the CMI appears to be an embryonic Asian Monetary Fund (AMF). The key issue for the United States is the degree of coordination of lending conditionality between the IMF and a potential AMF. If the AMF were to lend under loose or absent conditionality, the large pool of public money could fuel moral hazard and eventually contribute to the collapse of the globally oriented IMF. Currently, only 20 percent of CMI funds can be drawn before triggering IMF linkage. Nevertheless, theoretically this means that the financing that some Asian countries can now access through the CMI mechanism exceeds their IMF quota. Today, the CMI appears to be consistent with the existing global financial architecture. But Asian countries possess roughly $3 trillion in official reserves, around 50 percent of the world total. If the political will is there, Asia has the financial wherewithal to go its own way. Whether it will depends significantly on the capacity of Japan and China to act cooperatively.

Trade Issues

Similar tensions between global and regional institutions exist with respect to trade policy. As in the macroeconomic sphere, the United States faces the challenge of prioritizing its efforts between multilateral, regional, and bilateral initiatives; and evaluating its interests vis-à-vis Asian regional initiatives.

The United States faces the challenge of prioritizing its efforts between multilateral, regional, and bilateral initiatives; and evaluating its interests vis-à-vis Asian regional initiatives.

The World Trade Organization (WTO) is the centerpiece of U.S. trade policy. All major Asian countries are members. The organization's ongoing negotiations, the Doha Development Round, has stalled for a variety of reasons: a complex negotiating agenda; the increasing assertiveness of a number of middle powers; and political weakness among traditional major powers which has made compromise, particularly on the central issue of agriculture, more difficult. On agriculture, Asia has no coherent regional interest. Some Asian countries, such as Japan and South Korea, have some of the world's most inefficient and protected agricultural sectors; while others such as Thailand, Indonesia, and the Philippines are members of the Cairns Group of self-identified, non-subsidizing agricultural exporters.

The prospects for successfully concluding the round have been dimmed even further by the expiration of "fast-track" negotiating authority for the president. (The "fast-track" procedure pre-commits Congress to a simple up/down vote without amendment within a specified time frame, without which successful negotiation of a global trade accord would probably be impossible.) The next administration will need to approach Congress immediately to secure fast-track authority to attempt to salvage Doha. Yet, U.S. credibility was dealt a potentially fatal blow in April 2008 by the congressional decision to alter the fast track rules ex post in the case of the Colombian Free Trade Agreement. Some in Congress argue that the Colombian case is unique and should not set a precedent for other fast track cases (including KORUS); but what matters in this context is not attitudes on Capitol Hill, but rather the reactions of foreign governments — as they will be the ultimate arbiters of how badly Congress has damaged U.S. negotiating credibility.

Stasis at the WTO has encouraged preferential trade initiatives. APEC is the most prominent such scheme in Asia. Its membership established the goal of free trade in the region by 2020, with the developed countries of the group completely freeing their trade by 2010. But this commitment has foundered for a variety of reasons, including the lack of any enforcement mechanism. As a consequence, APEC has devolved into more of a consultative organization to encourage trade and investment facilitation, and an annual opportunity for heads of government to meet.

As trade liberalization has stalled at the global and regional levels, action has naturally shifted toward more limited sub-regional and bilateral initiatives. The Association of Southeast Asian Nations or ASEAN has led the way, rhetorically at least, in trying to place its own sub-regional ASEAN FTA (AFTA), as the center of a hub-and-spoke system. The United States successfully concluded a free trade agreement with Singapore, but negotiations with several other Asian countries have stalled.

In light of the deteriorating political environment in the United States, it is unclear whether KORUS will ever be ratified. Confronting this situation will be at the top of the agenda of the incoming administration. The U.S. Congress has never failed to ratify a bilateral trade pact and failure to implement KORUS would be a terrible blow to U.S.-Korea relations, U.S. standing in Asia, and the U.S. role in global trade policy.

The U.S. Congress has never failed to ratify a bilateral trade pact and failure to implement KORUS would be a terrible blow to U.S.-Korea relations, U.S. standing in Asia, and the U.S. role in global trade policy.

As a post-industrial economy, the United States strongly emphasizes trans-border issues such as investment and services, which are more difficult to negotiate than more traditional bilateral measures such as tariffs, which are the focus of intra-Asian deals. The U.S. penchant for loading labor standards and environmental concerns into these agreements creates a situation in which negotiating an FTA with the United States is more challenging than with other potential partners, particularly China.

Through the process of diverting trade from globally efficient producers to less efficient – though preferentially favored – producers in signatory countries, preferential agreements can potentially harm both signatories and third parties alike. The prospect of being adversely affected by discriminatory deals in Asia (especially those involving the large economies of Northeast Asia) might possibly constitute a "wake-up call" for the U.S. Congress, forcing the United States to reassess its stance and adopt a more forthcoming posture. Korea, for example, is in the midst of an FTA negotiation with the European Union.

The most constructive course would be to re-emphasize global liberalization through the WTO and thereby reduce the value of preferential deals. Alternatively the United States could play tit-for-tat — either by trying to match or join the Asian initiatives, or by further expanding its own web of preferential agreements. Either option assumes that the United States has the political capacity to liberalize trade.

Aid

While commercial relations form the core of U.S. economic engagement with Asia, development assistance will continue to be an important aspect of diplomacy toward lower-income Asian countries.

While commercial relations form the core of U.S. economic

engagement with Asia, development assistance will continue

to be an important aspect of diplomacy toward lower-income

Asian countries.

Within the multilateral development banks, the United States has advocated re-focusing assistance toward the lowest income countries and away from middle income countries as well as urging programmatic and procedural changes. Unsurprisingly, these ideas have not been received with particular enthusiasm by non-favored recipients and some other donors. One issue is how to "graduate" China from eligibility. It is a poor country, yet it also includes pockets of considerable wealth, has launched a manned rocket into orbit, and demonstrates ample ability to attract private capital.

At the bilateral level, the U.S. approach is embodied in the Millennium Challenge Account (MCA), administered by a government corporation, the Millennium Challenge Corporation. Five Asian countries – Indonesia, Mongolia, the Philippines, Timor-Leste, and Vanuatu – are currently MCA eligible. Some Asian countries (such as Vietnam) meet the MCA income level criterion, but fail on other criteria (typically regarding governance). Countries that do not qualify for the MCA will remain eligible for other sorts of bilateral assistance. HIV-AIDS and public health programs, as well as pollution control and "green" assistance, which are not subject to MCA strictures, will probably account for a growing share of future U.S. foreign assistance.

Lastly, food issues, a staple of development policy a generation or two ago, had in large part dropped off the development agenda until the explosion in world prices in 2007-08. American policies and leadership in this arena will have a significant impact on a number of the poorer countries in Asia.

Recommendations and Conclusions

The economic policy agenda of the incoming administration will be shaped by financial market and macroeconomic developments that are by definition unknowable at present. Its ability to respond constructively to some of these challenges, particularly in the trade sphere, will depend to a large extent on electoral outcomes in November 2008.

In the trade arena, three issues will require immediate attention: the re-establishment of fast-track negotiating authority for the president, the completion of the Doha Round, and the passage of the KORUS FTA. The highest priority should be placed on passing KORUS, if only because the cost of failure to do so, in both economic and broader diplomatic terms, is so large.

The administration will also face a series of ongoing issues where the risks are longer-term in nature, and the common recommendation is "first, do no harm." This applies to regulation of financial markets in the United States; regulation of foreign investment in the U.S. (particularly by SWFs); and the multifaceted (macroeconomic, financial, and trade and investment) economic engagement with China, which will be the most politically sensitive bilateral relationship over the next four years.

In the trade arena, three issues will require immediate attention: the re-establishment of fast-track negotiating authority for the president, the completion of the Doha Round, and the passage of the KORUS FTA.

Finally, in the area of least immediate domestic political sensitivity, the administration will have to formulate a coherent strategy for responding to the emerging regional and sub-regional policy initiatives within Asia in both the financial and trade spheres. With respect to finance, first priority should be on ensuring that the expanding regional initiatives are compatible with the broader global financial architecture; and secondly on pursuing the specifics of the U.S. policy agenda through institutions such as the ADB. Analogously, in the trade arena the emphasis should be on shaping the development of preferential schemes in ways that are compatible with broader global rules, and dealing with — by pre-emption, emulation, or countermeasures — preferential schemes that would harm U.S. interests.

AMERICA'S ROLE IN ENGAGING WITH ASIA'S NEW REGIONALISM

Ellen L. Frost

Issue: The East Asian financial crisis in 1997 gave renewed impetus to efforts by regional countries to forge new organizational arrangements that in some cases excluded the United States, as in the case of the ASEAN Plus Three and the East Asian Summit. The United States for its part has been ambivalent about the importance it should attach to full participation in these institutions. How should a new U.S. administration position itself on this question?

Introduction

Asian regionalism has acquired new momentum. In the name of closer integration and "community-building," Asian governments have forged new organizations that encompass as many as 16 governments, including India and Australia. But they exclude the region's most prominent power – the United States.

China, already the region's number-one economic locomotive, has become a constructive and adept practitioner of regional diplomacy. By contrast, the United States is widely perceived to be distracted, indifferent, and increasingly protectionist. Most Asian leaders are hoping that a new president will actively re-engage with their region.

How should a new U.S. administration position itself on Asian regionalism, and specifically on pan-Asian organizations? Should it revitalize U.S. participation in the Asia Pacific Economic Cooperation forum (APEC)? Is it worth devoting high-level travel time and attention to a series of dialogues in a relatively peaceful part of the world? This chapter makes the case for substantial re-engagement on all fronts.

The long-range goal of the Asian integration movement is not political union, but a loosely defined "East Asian Community" of nation-states. It would consist of three broad pillars: economic, security, and socio-cultural.[1]

The architecture that Asian governments have erected to span their vast territory can be thought of as two circles, both centered on the 10-member Association of Southeast Asian Nations (ASEAN). Established in 1967, ASEAN is led – slowly and disjointedly – by its five founders: Indonesia, Malaysia, the Philippines, Singapore, and Thailand.[2] The first circle is ASEAN plus Japan, China, and South Korea (ASEAN Plus 3), which coalesced in 1997.

India, Australia, and New Zealand belong to the second, somewhat wider circle, the 16-member East Asian Summit (EAS) grouping (ASEAN Plus 6), which has held annual meetings at the head of s tate level since 2005.[3] (The term "East Asia" has evolved from a geographic expression to a political construct.)[4] ASEAN Plus 3 is far more institutionalized than the East Asian Summit.

Linking these disparate governments is a "noodle bowl" of mostly bilateral free trade agreements (most of which are unenforceable and riddled with exceptions) and a network of bilateral currency swap agreements. Another bond is ASEAN's signature foreign policy document, the Treaty of Amity and Cooperation (TAC), which enshrines the normative basis for Asian community-building. The TAC is not so much a treaty as a non-binding declaration of principles, including non-interference in internal affairs, renunciation of the threat or use of force, and the peaceful settlement of disputes. China was the first non-ASEAN country to sign the TAC; all other Asian governments and all external powers with significant interests in the region have followed suit, except the United States.

China was the first non-ASEAN country to sign the TAC;

all other Asian governments and all external powers with

significant interests in the region have followed suit, except the

United States.

ASEAN members are also the creators of the ASEAN Regional Forum (ARF), a regional security dialogue. Unlike ASEAN Plus 3 and the East Asian Summit group, the ARF includes the United States, the European Union, Russia, India, China, Japan, and others. Neither of the region's two main potential flashpoints – North Korea and the Taiwan Strait – is ever on the agenda, but other security topics are aired and discussed.

For many Asian governments, the very process of regional integration is a goal in itself, no matter how time-consuming it is and whether or not it achieves near-term results. In a once-violent region that lacks a regional security organization, ASEAN Plus 3, the East Asian Summit process, and the ARF provide some degree of "soft" security by reinforcing peaceful norms, cushioning bilateral tensions, and facilitating personal communication and trust. The new architecture embeds China in a web of committees and dialogues, opens doors to India, and helps channel rivalry in constructive directions.

The Role of China

Although the balance of power in Asia is stable, the balance of influence is tilting in favor of China.[5] Asian leaders calculate that enmeshing China in a web of agreements and dialogues encourages peaceful and cooperative behavior and a greater degree of openness. For their part, Chinese leaders see an opportunity to expand China's influence, subtly marginalize Japan, consolidate the diplomatic isolation of Taiwan, and establish a constructive counterweight to the U.S. presence without antagonizing Washington.

Asian leaders calculate that enmeshing China in a web of agreements and dialogues encourages peaceful and cooperative behavior and a greater degree of openness.

The pan-Asian organizations embodying Asia's new regionalism both reflect and dilute China's new role. China, typically supported by Malaysia, favors ASEAN Plus 3, where it tends to prevail in the competition for influence. But Japan and Singapore fought successfully to include India, Australia, and New Zealand in the East Asian Summit grouping to balance China's weight. The result satisfies no one completely, but the vague, open-ended nature of the process allows plenty of room for maneuver and thus corresponds to Asia's fluid strategic environment.

U.S. Policy toward Regional Integration

Postwar U.S. policy toward regionalism in various parts of the world has reflected the judgment that regional integration is consistent with national, regional, and global U.S. interests — with or without U.S. participation — provided that it meets certain reasonable and publicly articulated conditions. In the U.S. view, regional integration should not be designed to undermine global institutions, damage security ties between the United States and a major ally, or permit domination by a power hostile to the United States. It should be consistent with market-oriented trade and investment policies, with a goal of trade creation rather than trade diversion, and accompanied by compensation for any lost U.S. exports. Judging from repeated assurances from Asian leaders, and assuming that the U.S.-China relationship remains stable and not antagonistic, the organizations that reflect Asia's new regionalism appear to satisfy these long-standing U.S. criteria.

Conscious of China's gains and aware of accusations of neglect and indifference, Bush administration officials switched from a "wait and see" attitude toward Asian regionalism to cautious approval. Ever since the creation of the East Asian Summit in 2005, however, they have put special emphasis on achieving synergy and avoiding duplication and inefficiency. Many of them see the integration movement as merely a series of "talk shops" and photo opportunities, with few if any deliverables. U.S. officials see transnational challenges and threats in Asia that Asian governments have barely begun to tackle effectively, such as crime, disease, and pollution.

This attitude is understandable (and indeed shared by some Asian elites), but it overlooks the need to build trust and manage key power relationships. In their own way, Asians, particularly Southeast Asians, are performing this task quite well.

The Legacy of Neglect

By focusing so heavily on the Middle East and anti-terrorism, the Bush administration has largely excluded itself from high-level regional diplomacy in Asia. The most serious blow to America's reputation as a concerned and responsive partner in the region, however, occurred when the Clinton administration refused to come to the aid of Thailand and Indonesia during the financial crisis of 1997-98 – only three and a half years after helping Mexico during a similar crisis. Clinton administration officials were also identified with conditions imposed by the International Monetary Fund (IMF) that some judged to be unduly austere, especially in Indonesia. Asians still talk about this experience.

The most serious blow to America's reputation as a concerned and responsive partner in the region, however, occurred when the Clinton administration refused to come to the aid of Thailand and Indonesia during the financial crisis of 1997-98 – only three and a half years after helping Mexico during a similar crisis.

The aftermath of 9/11 was another setback to effective, two-way, high-level engagement with Asia. President Bush harped incessantly on antiterrorism and "homeland security," engaged in tin-ear moralizing instead of listening, hammered on North Korea's nuclear weapons programs while downplaying other Asian security concerns, and launched a war in Iraq. Unlike China, which offered a trade agreement with ASEAN as a whole, the Bush administration made free-trade offers that were exclusively bilateral.[6]

Unlike China, which offered a trade agreement with ASEAN as a whole, the Bush administration made free-trade offers that were exclusively bilateral.

If this self-exclusion from regional diplomacy continues, nothing drastic will happen soon, but Washington's voice will continue to lose resonance. Japan will likely become further marginalized, Southeast Asians will face limits on exercising their national sovereignty, and unfettered access to U.S. bases could well become problematic.

Recommendations and Conclusions: What Should Change — and What Shouldn't

1. Listen, Don't Preach

To regain a rightful place in regional diplomacy, the United Sates should begin by taking Asian regionalism seriously —

listen to its various voices, try to understand what challenges Asian governments face, and grasp its internal and external political dynamics. What Americans see as duplication and overlap, Asians see as safety valves.

To regain a rightful place in regional diplomacy, the United Sates should begin by taking Asian regionalism seriously —

listen to its various voices, try to understand what challenges

Asian governments face, and grasp its internal and external

political dynamics. What Americans see as duplication and

overlap, Asians see as safety valves.

President Bush's assertion in 2001 that members of the international community "are either with us or against us" in the struggle against terrorism struck Asians as both absolutist and highly self-centered. Low-key efforts by Deputy Secretaries of State Robert Zoellick and John Negroponte, in addition to Treasury Secretary Henry Paulson partially repaired the U.S. profile, but much more listening is in order.

2. Devise a Coordinated Interagency Strategy toward Asia as a Region

For at least the last 10 years, and arguably much longer, U.S. policies toward Asia have been compartmentalized by issue and by country, with little attention paid to Asia's new regionalism and even less interagency coordination. Region-wide economic and security priorities are rarely discussed in the same room.

The starting point for a coordinated strategy should be the recognition that re-engaging with Asia as a region is a strategic imperative. Asia is the home of a rising power and the locus of important U.S. interests. No major global problem can be solved without some degree of cooperation with — and among – half of the world's population. For these reasons the United States must re-engage; it cannot afford to do otherwise.

No major global problem can be solved without some degree of cooperation with — and among – half of the world's population. For these reasons the United States must re-engage; it cannot afford to do otherwise.

---

3. Re-Engage with ASEAN at the Highest Level

Both the Clinton and Bush administrations resisted U.S.-ASEAN summit meetings because they believed that such discussions would legitimize the government of Myanmar (formerly known as Burma). This was a case of the tail wagging the dog. In 2007, President Bush agreed to attend a U.S.-ASEAN summit, but he subsequently cancelled it. He sought to reschedule, but to change the location to Texas; not surprisingly, ASEAN governments demurred.

The new administration should quickly seek to reschedule a U.S.-ASEAN summit. It is always difficult to persuade a U.S. president to travel overseas, especially to a place as far from Washington as Southeast Asia, when nothing very tangible will be announced. Engagement requires patient, personal effort. But as a means of bolstering sagging U.S. popularity and influence, there is no substitute for the personal relationships and political visibility associated with summitry. Indeed, the new administration should consider choosing Asia as the destination of the president's first overseas trip.

The new administration should consider choosing Asia as the destination of the president's first overseas trip.

Secretaries of State of both parties tend to get bogged down in the Middle East. They travel there frequently but do not seem to have time to go to Asia. Secretary of State Rice skipped two of the last four meetings of the ASEAN Regional Forum, which caused other foreign ministers to stay away or leave early. The new Secretary of State should make a point of attending the next forum.

In 2008, the Bush administration created the new position of Ambassador for ASEAN Affairs. This was a wise and welcome move, but unlike the U.S. Ambassador to the European

Union and various United Nations' entities, the new ambassador is "double-hatted" as a deputy assistant secretary and will
serve in Washington rather than Jakarta, where the ASEAN
Secretariat is located. The new administration should separate
the two positions and post the ambassador to ASEAN's headquarters in Jakarta.

4. Sign the Treaty of Amity and Cooperation (TAC)

The most direct way for the United States to re-engage with
Asia's new regionalism would be to sign the TAC, with appropriate caveats of the sort negotiated by Australia. These said
essentially that the TAC would not alter Australia's other treaty
and security commitments in the region. Since the TAC is only
a statement of principles and contains no restrictions on U.S.
deployments, the U.S. military posture would not be affected.
There are indications that Senate approval would not be
beyond reach.

*The most direct way for the United States to re-engage with
Asia's new regionalism would be to sign the TAC.*

The most important reason for signing the TAC is that doing
so would signify re-engagement in the regional competition for
influence. It would confirm that the United States is on a par
with other members of the EAS as a "good citizen" of the emerging Asian community. Signature alone is one of three stated
criteria for membership in the EAS, and the United States meets
the other two ("dialogue partner" status and significant economic

engagement). In addition, signature would symbolize respect for ASEAN's efforts to maintain stability in the region and underscore America's positive attitude and peaceful intentions.

Signature need *not* imply, however, that the United States will press to join the EAS; indeed, doing so would be perceived as (characteristically) aggressive. Such pressure would also create problems for ASEAN (for instance, what about Russia?). The United States is unique: not only is it located on the other side of the ocean, but – unlike other members of the EAS – it is also a global power with regional interests rather than primarily a regional power. If asked to join, however, the United States should accept, recognizing that membership requires a presidential trip. (Such a meeting would probably be timed to follow on the heels of the annual APEC summit.)

5. Reinvigorate and Fully Fund U.S. Participation in APEC and Other Trans-Pacific Activities

APEC, a trans-Pacific organization championed by the first Clinton administration, lost altitude in the mid-1990s and has languished ever since. In addition to re-engaging with pan-Asian organizations, the new administration should revitalize U.S. participation in APEC by upgrading and fully funding U.S. representation.

APEC offers a constructive strategic balancing-weight to ASEAN Plus 3 and other pan-Asian organizations. The United States should exercise leadership by rejuvenating the 1993-94 APEC vision of "free and open trade and investment" while accommodating the needs of other members. Although APEC as a whole is large and unwieldy, the United States can begin to put this vision into practice by concluding agreements with subgroups such as the "P-4" (Singapore, Chile, New Zealand, and Brunei) and perhaps others. An initial priority could be strengthening joint measures to combat narcotics trafficking; another could be energy.

One issue that will face the new administration is that India is seeking to join APEC. The Bush administration and other governments parried this idea, noting that membership is currently frozen (until 2010). Another objection is that India still maintains the highest tariffs of any major developing country and has yet to demonstrate a meaningful commitment to "free and open trade and investment." Moreover, some fear that Indian membership would elicit a similar request from Pakistan. From a strategic perspective, however, Indian membership would be helpful. Some kind of compromise may need to be found – for example, initial observer status followed by a long transition. The U.S. position should be discussed and coordinated with others — particularly Australia, Japan, China, and Singapore.

In addition to APEC, exerting more leadership and upgrading participation in other trans-Pacific organizations should be a strategic priority. Particular attention should be paid to increasing the size and travel budgets of civilian U.S. government agencies participating in such meetings. Doing so would partially rectify the huge imbalance between military and non-military foreign policy tools and highlight the large reservoir of U.S. skills applicable to non-traditional threats.

Most U.S. military leaders stationed in Hawaii and the western Pacific have a good grasp of the nuances of Asian regionalism. The training and joint military exercises sponsored by the U.S. Pacific Command are valuable diplomatic assets and should be continued. Washington policymakers should respond quickly and appropriately to remove any obstacles identified by U.S. officers, such as excessive classification of whole military systems and technologies.

6. Avoid Making Asians Take Sides

The new administration should avoid anything that puts Asians in a position where they have to choose between China and the United States, between China and Japan, or between democracies on the rim of East Asia (especially Japan, Australia, and India) and China and its mainland neighbors. Bilateral or trilateral discussions with fellow democracies are fine, but they should be matched by talks with others. Above all, the new administration should eschew policies that conjure up encirclement or containment of China, such as a "League of Democracies" or a "Cold War of Ideas." A far better approach would be to improve the functioning of our own democracy, thereby setting an example.

The Bush administration came into office vowing to restore a strong relationship with Japan and tilt somewhat away from China. Since then, however, it has established and maintained constructive relationships with both. The new administration should continue on this course.

7. Revive America's "Soft Power" Assets

Instead of seeking membership in pan-Asian organizations, the new administration should respond to the shifting balance of influence by drawing on U.S. strengths. First, it should address America's own blemishes ("Physician, heal thyself"). Second, working closely with Congress, the new administration should

greatly expand the number of scholarships and mid-level training opportunities, facilitate visa applications, further open its
markets, and restore the spirit of generosity and openness that
inspired earlier generations of Asians. If U.S. leaders engage with
Asia's new regionalism in a supportive and open-minded way,
Asians will welcome a U.S. presence – not at every table, but
definitely under their roof.

---

[1] East Asia Vision Group, "Towards an East Asian Community," ASEAN Secretariat, 2001.

[2] The other members of ASEAN are Brunei, Cambodia, Laos, Myanmar, and Vietnam.

[3] Separately, and for different reasons, in 2001 China established the Shanghai Cooperation
Organization, which includes Russia, Kazakhstan, Kyrgyzstan, Tajikistan, and Uzbekistan.

[4] Singapore's Goh Chok Tong makes this point repeatedly. See, for example, "Towards an
East Asian Renaissance," February 6, 2006, Speech at the 4th Asia-Pacific Roundtable.
Singapore. Available at http://app.sprinter.gov.sg/data/pr/20060206999.htm.

[5] For more on this theme, see Ellen L. Frost, James J. Przystup, and Phillip C. Saunders,
"China's Rising Influence in Asia: Implications for U.S. Policy," Strategic Forum 231,
Washington, DC: Institute for National Strategic Studies, National Defense University,
April 2008.

[6] However, in August 2007 the Bush administration signed a Trade and Investment
Framework Agreement (TIFA) with ASEAN. In U.S. trade policy, a TIFA is a prerequisite to
a free-trade agreement.

ENERGY SECURITY IN THE ASIA-PACIFIC REGION AND POLICY FOR THE NEW U.S. ADMINISTRATION

Mikkal Herberg

Issue: The fast-growing Asian economies have intensified the global demand for vital resources. The high price of oil has been one of the consequences. The United States has a fundamental interest in ensuring that the competition for these resources, especially energy, is conducted within the framework of accepted international ground rules. What approach should the next U.S. administration adopt, in its relations with Asian countries, toward safeguarding access to vital energy supplies?

Introduction

Global energy markets have experienced an unprecedented period of tightening over the past eight years as oil prices have climbed from $20 per barrel in 2000 to $140 as of this writing. Consequently, high prices and a growing sense of supply scarcity have led to a range of new tensions among the major oil import-ing countries in the Asia-Pacific region over energy security and market access to global energy supplies. Rising *energy nationalism* in the region has fed an atmosphere of "zero-sum" national com-petition over access to energy supplies and control over trans-portation corridors. *Resource nationalism* among the major export-ing countries further aggravates the consuming countries' fears over supplies. Global energy markets are being politicized and balkanized while the risks of supply disruptions are growing, as the importing countries are competing among themselves rather than working together to pursue their mutual interests in more stable global energy markets.

Energy angst in the United States, China, India, Japan, and the rest of oil-importing Asia has also added new tensions to an already complex Asian strategic environment. Energy rivalries have become a factor in the historic power transition occurring in Asia; featuring the interplay of the rise of China and India, Japan's efforts to maintain its pivotal role in the region, Russia's efforts to recapture some of its influence in Northeast Asia, and U.S. efforts to maintain its role in maintaining a strategic balance of power in the region. U.S.-China energy disagreements on the CNOOC-Unocal acquisition and China's expansive energy diplomacy, Sino-Japanese energy conflicts around access to Russian oil pipelines and over offshore natural gas fields, China-India suspicions of each other's energy and pipeline diplomacy, and lingering disagreements in Southeast Asia over maritime borders and ownership of energy supplies (as well as how to manage security in key energy transit sea-lanes) have all added new tensions to a number of important bilateral relationships. Strategic disagreements, in turn, are spilling back over into energy relations and undermining efforts at energy cooperation.

The drift toward mistrust and national competition over energy can only be reversed by turning energy into a source of regional cooperation and competitive markets rather than national competition and politicized markets.

The drift toward mistrust and national competition over energy can only be reversed by turning energy into a source of regional cooperation and competitive markets rather than national competition and politicized markets. The United States, China, Japan, India, and other Southeast Asian countries have fundamental *mutual energy security* interests in stable global energy markets, secure and free access to energy supplies, reasonable prices, reliable energy transit, and an environmentally sustainable energy future. These countries need to find collective ways to build trust, manage and contain the impulse toward energy competition, begin working together to promote new supplies, build new regional energy infrastructure, undermine the predatory market power of the producing states, and cooperate on developing a more environmentally sustainable long-term energy future. Without such a change, the United States and the Asian region are very likely to face continued high and volatile energy prices, unstable supplies, growing dependence on unreliable political regimes, more politicized energy markets, and ultimately disastrous environmental and climate outcomes.

Recommendations

Changing these increasingly competitive energy dynamics to more cooperative ones will require much stronger and more creative U.S. leadership, in addition to some re-ordering of strategic priorities. It will take similarly creative political leadership in Beijing, Tokyo, and New Delhi and greater openness to fundamental policy change. Efforts by the new U.S. administration need to be rooted in fundamental mutual interests regarding global energy development and use.

Three principles should be the touchstones of Asian regional energy security policy for the next U.S. administration: 1) promoting regional energy cooperation, 2) enhancing efforts to manage chronic areas of tension, and 3) reducing demand growth to take pressure off tight global energy supply conditions.

Three principles should be the touchstones of Asian regional energy security policy for the next U.S. administration: 1) promoting regional energy cooperation, 2) enhancing efforts to manage chronic areas of tension, and 3) reducing demand growth to take pressure off tight global energy supply conditions.

PROMOTING REGIONAL ENERGY COOPERATION

Managing energy competition in the region needs to be approached in a coordinated fashion at the regional, multilateral, and bilateral levels. Regionally, the United States needs to lead the development of a strategic regional energy dialogue on common energy concerns with the initial goal of de-politicizing the issue of energy security. Energy has become an important strategic concern in the region; it is now part of the "high politics" of national security rather than the "low politics" of domestic energy policy. The United States is both the sole strategic superpower and, at the same time, the superpower of the energy world. No regional energy security dialogue can succeed without strong U.S. leadership and commitment. China is becoming a global energy superpower; India is becoming a new regional energy power; Japan is the second-largest oil importer in the world and the global superpower of energy efficiency; Russia has become the largest energy exporter in the world; and Southeast Asia is among the most important maritime energy transit regions on the globe.

The United States is both the sole strategic superpower and, at the same time, the superpower of the energy world. No regional energy security dialogue can succeed without strong U.S. leadership and commitment.

This regional energy dialogue should be aimed at confidence-building and improving mutual trust regarding the energy intentions and policies toward supply access among the key powers in the region. Its initial focus should be on common interests in maintaining stability in global energy markets and supporting market competition for access to supplies rather than state-led exclusive energy deals; and on demonstrating that in a globalized energy market no country can achieve energy security unilaterally. There is only one global oil market and stability in that market can be achieved only through global collaboration. As this dialogue matures, it can potentially begin to support regional oil and natural gas production and pipeline transportation solutions that can only be achieved in the context of a regional coordinating organization. This forum would also provide a better means for discussing collective regional approaches to security in the key energy sea lanes of communication (SLOCs) of Southeast Asia; and resolving a multitude of overlapping maritime claims in the South China Sea where the potential for energy resources risks inflaming bilateral territorial disputes. This dialogue should be coordinated with a broader effort to evolve a strategic Northeast Asian regional forum out of the Six-Party Talks.

Multilaterally, the next administration should make it a goal to bring China and India more directly into the global institutions that manage oil market disruptions, most importantly the International Energy Agency (IEA).

Multilaterally, the next administration should make it a goal to bring China and India more directly into the global institutions that manage oil market disruptions, most importantly the International Energy Agency (IEA). The IEA was established in the 1970s as a mechanism for managing supply disruptions and promoting energy cooperation and efficiency. However, the sources of growth in world oil demand have shifted sharply away from the industrial countries toward the developing countries, with China and India alone expected to account for over 40 percent of global oil demand growth over the next two decades. Today the world's global emergency oil management system does not include two of the six largest oil consuming countries. Since China and India are not members of the OECD, the U.S. and Japan need to lead an effort to find creative ways to incorporate them into the IEA's emergency management system. The recent U.S. announcement of its support for China's membership in the IEA is only a start. The new head of the IEA, Nobuo Tanaka, is from Japan and has a mandate to develop stronger relationships with China and India.

Involvement in the IEA brings with it exposure to expertise on energy efficiency, demand management, technology, and policy-making expertise that would be extremely valuable in accelerating the "learning curve" of energy policymakers in China and India.

Today the world's global emergency oil management system does not include two of the six largest oil consuming countries.

Bilaterally, the U.S. should raise the level of importance of and commitment to current energy dialogues with China and India, the region's key growing energy consuming countries. There is enormous scope for cooperation on a range of issues including moderating demand growth, improving energy efficiency, promoting diffusion of energy saving technology, and reducing pollution and carbon emissions. China and India alone are expected to account for over 40 percent of the increase in oil consumption, 75 percent of the increase in world coal consumption, and 45 percent of the increase in global carbon emissions over the next two decades. The United States holds regular energy dialogues with both countries but these are not sufficiently ambitious to raise the importance of energy issues to the level of strategic cooperation. They tend to remain at a technical expert level, move at a glacial pace, and have almost no discernable impact on energy and oil demand growth. They are rapidly falling behind the level of effort and financial commitment that is needed. The dialogues need to be given higher-level political support and far more resources to meet the challenge.

China and India alone are expected to account for over 40

percent of the increase in oil consumption, 75 percent of the

increase in world coal consumption, and 45 percent of the

increase in global carbon emissions over the next two decades.

MANAGING AREAS OF TENSION

Even assuming significantly enhanced Asian energy cooperation in the future, a number of tensions concerning the competitive energy diplomacy of key players and access strategies of the region's major powers to oil and gas supplies in sensitive countries are likely to continue. These tensions will need to be carefully managed.

This is particularly important vis-à-vis China. U.S.-China energy relations remain burdened by mistrust and suspicion emanating from a series of disputes over the attempted CNOOC acquisition of Unocal[1]; U.S. perceptions of China's national oil companies' investments abroad as predatory and state-driven; and China's energy involvement in numerous problem states such as Iran, Sudan, and Myanmar (formerly known as Burma). Currently, discussions with China are handled through the bilateral U.S.-China Energy Dialogue led by Department of Energy and as part of the U.S.-China Strategic Economic Dialogue (SED) led by the U.S. Treasury Secretary. The SED includes energy on the agenda, but this dialogue is not well-suited to discussing energy security in a strategic context. It is an *economic* dialogue rather than a *strategic* dialogue. Energy needs to be put on the strategic agenda in high-level executive bilateral discussions, such as the State Department's continuing Senior Dialogue which emerged from the Zoellick U.S.-China Strategic Dialogue.

In sharp contrast, the Bush administration has sought to use high-level energy cooperation, specifically the proposed nuclear energy deal, as a means to promote stronger U.S.-India strategic relations. Nevertheless, three issues loom in U.S.-India energy relations that need to be managed carefully to avoid new tensions. First, India shows every intention of expanding its energy ties with Iran. Second, India's efforts to develop a large new pipeline to import natural gas from Myanmar are also likely to raise tensions. Finally, India's energy investments in Sudan will remain a potential point of disagreement (although U.S. attention on Sudan energy investments has thus far been focused on China, given its role on the U.N. Security Council and its capability to frustrate U.S. efforts to pressure Sudan's government over human rights violations).

Strategic disagreements over energy investments are also appearing in U.S.-Japan relations, most notably over Japan's recent oil field investment plans in Iran which provoked serious opposition from the U.S. As in the case of India, the historically strong U.S.-Japan alliance means that these energy disagreements are likely to have a limited impact on bilateral relations. The case of both India and Japan contrasts sharply with the case of China, where a broad and intensifying U.S.-China strategic rivalry tends to exaggerate the negative impact on bilateral relations of a range of global energy disagreements and conflicting policy interests.

Managing demand growth

Underlying the increasingly nationalistic competition over access to future oil supplies is the growing mismatch between strong oil demand growth and a dysfunctional global supply situation. Due to a range of political constraints and instability in key producing regions, supplies are not responding to high prices; and the longer-term global oil supply outlook is extremely precarious. Hence, the *most effective* energy security strategy for the region is to collaborate in addressing the domestic demand side of the energy equation to ease the global supply squeeze. Oil demand in the U.S., China, and India is among the most important factors behind rising world oil prices. However, these countries are making only minimal efforts to slow demand growth. Persistently high demand in the context of a precarious global supply picture delivers the economic prosperity of all the major importers into the hands of unstable or unresponsive producer countries.

Hence, self-help is critical to reducing the competition for supplies. Demand is the element of the equation that the United States, China, and India can control if they can summon the political will to do so; and is the one thing that the Organization of the Petroleum Exporting Countries (OPEC) and other major producers, such as Russia, cannot control. The effort requires both regional cooperation and domestic strategies. What is needed is no less than an *Asia-Pacific Strategic Energy Efficiency Initiative* — a cooperative multilateral effort, led by the United States, China, India, and Japan. Japan can play a critical role in this by contributing its policy expertise, experience, and technology in reducing oil demand growth.

Presently, Chinese and Indian energy policies are heavily biased toward supply-side and statist solutions to energy shortages, rather than demand management and market-oriented strategies.

Subsidized energy pricing, inefficient state-owned monopolies in the energy industry, selective limits on foreign investment in energy, bureaucratic interference in the energy sector, cross-subsidies, and opaque and unstable policies all work to slow new energy investments, delay efficiency improvements, subsidize high-demand growth, and undermine the introduction of new, energy saving technology. Stronger domestic commitments in China and India to energy market and pricing reform, diversification, and efficiency can be supported and encouraged by bilateral and multilateral cooperation; along with financial and technical assistance, in which the United States and Japan need to take a lead role.

Self-help is critical to reducing the competition for supplies. Demand is the element of the equation that the United States, China, and India can control if they can summon the political will to do so; and is the one thing that the Organization of the Petroleum Exporting Countries (OPEC) and other major producers, such as Russia, cannot control. The effort requires both regional cooperation and domestic strategies. What is needed is no less than an 'Asia-Pacific Strategic Energy Efficiency Initiative'— a cooperative multilateral effort, led by the United States, China, India, and Japan.

U.S. energy policies, likewise, are heavily biased toward supply-side solutions while, at the same time, policies to slow demand growth have been feeble and timid. As a result, the United States has been a serious laggard on energy efficiency. For example, the U.S. consumes 80 percent more oil per capita than Japan and twice that of the European Union. Both the U.S. and Japan have much to offer regarding clean coal technology development and diffusion. The U.S. and Japan can also offer experience, assistance, and encouragement on natural gas development and markets.

An enormous improvement in domestic energy efficiency needs to become a central strategic goal in the United States, China, and India. Policies need to target oil and the transportation sector; but also coal, since it poses great environmental and climate threats. It will not be easy given the common energy pathologies in China, India, and the United States, particularly the supply-side bias of policymakers and powerful vested interests in these countries. The effort will also have to overcome fragmented and unfocused energy policymaking systems in all three countries, a lack of effective implementation policies, and powerful political resistance to paying higher energy costs.

An enormous improvement in domestic energy efficiency needs to become a central strategic goal in the United States, China, and India. Policies need to target oil and the transportation sector; but also coal, since it poses great environmental and climate threats.

Conclusions

A fundamental shift toward promoting regional energy cooperation, managing the geopolitical tensions in our current approaches
to energy security, and improving energy efficiency will take
courageous political leadership by the new administration in
Washington, D.C., but also in Beijing, New Delhi, and Tokyo.
Raising energy issues to a strategic policy level will be the biggest
hurdle. Nevertheless, without such a shift, all the political rhetoric
in Washington D.C., Beijing, New Delhi, and Tokyo about
achieving greater energy security will be so much arm-waving.
Without this change, we are likely to face continuing chronically
high and volatile world oil and energy prices, unstable supplies,
growing dependence on unstable political regimes, more politicized energy markets, and ultimately disastrous environmental
and climate outcomes.

---

[1] Unocal was eventually purchased and acquired by the Chevron Corporation.

ASIA'S ENVIRONMENTAL CRISIS: WHY THE U.S. SHOULD CARE AND WHAT IT SHOULD DO

Elizabeth Economy

Issue: The rapid pace of economic development in China, India, and other Asian countries is producing massive environmental degradation, including polluted water supplies, unhealthy air, toxic wastes, and depleted forests. Are there policies the United States and other developed countries could pursue, in their own self-interest, that would mitigate these problems without demanding that developing countries adopt politically unacceptable slower growth strategies? At the same time, the United States and China are now the world's largest producers of greenhouse emissions. Both have been reluctant to confront the economic costs and domestic consequences of stringently limiting these emissions. Is there an optimal way for the next U.S. administration to find a common approach with Asian countries on this question?

Introduction

Asia's extraordinary economic development over the past few decades has placed enormous pressure on the region's environment. Land degradation, acute water shortages, deforestation, and pollution are rising rapidly, and the region's natural resources are dwindling to unsustainable levels. Asia already has less water available per person than any other continent outside Antarctica, is home to 16 of the world's 20 most polluted cities,[1] and boasts the highest rates of deforestation and water erosion in the world. The next U.S. administration has a significant stake in Asia's environmental future. Asia's continued economic dynamism is a key contributor to the health of the U.S. and global economy; an environment-induced economic slowdown in the region would harm global growth. Polluted water and unsafe business practices in several Asian countries have brought contaminated fish and other food products to America's doorstep. Asia, and in particular China, is a leading contributor to global climate change as well as to transboundary air pollution that affects the health of the American people. And both China and India, like the developed world before them, are degrading the world's forests and natural environment in their global quest for resources to fuel their continued growth.

Addressing Asia's environmental crisis and its global implications will require the transformation of the region's development trajectory. China and India, as the region's largest developing economies with more than one-third of the world's population, matter most. They must move aggressively to conserve resources, implement advanced environmental technologies, and reform their domestic policy environments. The United States has a critical role to play in supporting this transformation through four measures: getting America's own environmental house in order; developing and implementing an effective means of transferring technology internationally; helping to establish the appropriate policy environment within China and India; and coordinating U.S. government efforts with U.S. multinational corporations and non-governmental institutions (NGOs), as well as with Japan and the European Union.

Understanding the Trends

U.S. policy must begin with a clear understanding of the emerging development and environmental challenges that Asia is confronting. The region is characterized by dramatically rising levels of urbanization and industrialization; weak local governance; significant and growing dependence on fossil fuels for energy; a rapidly expanding automobile sector; and a global quest for resources such as timber, oil, gas, and other commodities to fuel the region's continued growth.

Water Consumption, Pollution, and Public Health

As many as 635 million people in Asia lack access to safe water and 1.9 billion lack access to effective sanitation.[2] New urban and industrial centers are competing for shrinking water resources with traditional agricultural users, as energy demands for water are simultaneously increasing.[3] Rapid urbanization and industrialization also contribute to higher levels of water pollution. In India, all of the 14 major river systems are already seriously polluted.[4] In China, more than a quarter of the water that flows through the country's seven major river systems is considered unfit for even agriculture or industry. Waste treatment in both countries is minimal, and wastewater is often discharged directly to nearby rivers, lakes, or oceans. Most of the bodies of water in and around the urban centers of Asia's developing countries are now heavily contaminated.[5] Given estimates that the urban population in Asia is likely to balloon by 60 percent by 2025, with much of this growth occurring in China,[6] the scale of the impending challenge is enormous.

Dirty water and poor sanitation contribute to serious regional and global public health challenges. In China, diarrhea from polluted water is the leading cause of death in children under the age of five. In Southeast Asia in 2007, Dengue fever led to tens of thousands of people falling ill and hundreds of deaths. The disease, which is transmitted by a particular type of mosquito that thrives in stagnant water, can easily cross national boundaries through unknowing travelers. In addition, in the wake of the SARS (severe acute respiratory syndrome) pandemic in 2003, sewage and otherwise contaminated water from infected human feces were found to be potential transmitters of the virus.

Polluted water emanating from Asia's growing aquaculture industry also poses a global health threat. China produces 70 percent of the farmed fish in the world, but its poor environmental enforcement permits fisheries to use water that is contaminated by sewage, agricultural waste, and agricultural run-off such as pesticides. These fish farms in turn discharge wastewater that further pollutes the water supply. A number of shipments of contaminated seafood from China have been blocked over the past few years by the European Union, Japan, and the United States. (Similarly, soil contamination in China has led to the export of contaminated agricultural products.)

The rapidly rising demand for water in Asia is also contributing to heightened regional tensions. By 2050, some additional 1.8 billion people in Asia will need access to clean water and all the related necessities such as food and energy.[7] The World Bank estimates that at that time demand for water in India will exceed all supplies, and the Chinese government has forecast that by 2030 it will face an annual water shortfall of 53 trillion gallons — more than the country now consumes in a year.[8] As both countries increasingly seek to access water resources from the Himalayas and Tibetan Plateau to meet their water needs, they are also reshaping the water landscape and incurring conflict with their neighbors in Central, South, and Southeast Asia.[9]

Energy Consumption and Climate Change

Climate change may pose the greatest threat to the future of humankind in the 21st century. No country, including the United States, will escape unscathed and the potential impacts are devastating: a dramatic increase in the scope and scale of natural disasters, rising sea levels, extended periods of drought, radically shifting agricultural patterns, the introduction of new opportunities for pestilence, and the spread of deadly diseases.

For China and India, there is little good news in any climate change scenario. Already the Himalayan glaciers that support Asia's most critical rivers are melting at a faster rate than ever before. According to a 2007 survey, the glaciers could shrink by nearly a third by 2050 and up to half by 2090 at the current rate.[10] Food security for Asia, and as a result for the rest of the world, will be threatened. The Chinese government projects that by 2050, output of major crops such as wheat, rice and corn may decline by as much as 37 percent. In India, the government predicts a 30 percent drop in food-grain production, particularly wheat, by 2040.[11] Rising food prices and potentially even shortages in the United States would ensue as a result. Both countries are concerned about sea level rise. Coastal cities such as Shanghai could be submerged, forcing the reverse migration of tens of millions of people. India possesses a 7500 km-long, densely populated and low lying coastline; already 6000 people have had to relocate off two islands that have disappeared from the map. By the end of the century, some Indian analysts predict that there will be millions of migrants moving off the coastline.[12]

Today, China and India rank first and fifth, respectively, in terms of their contribution of the greenhouse gas carbon dioxide (the United States is second). Their relative and absolute contributions are expected to skyrocket over the next decades unless radical steps are taken to improve their energy efficiency, change the mix of their energy supply, and develop technologies that can capture and store carbon dioxide.[13] Senior Chinese leaders have indicated that the country's per capita emissions may well reach those of the United States by 2050, effectively erasing any benefit that might accrue from current global greenhouse gas mitigation efforts. India, which relies on coal for more than half of its overall energy, antici- pates that its emissions of carbon dioxide will jump from 1 billion tons to 5.5 billion tons by 2031, making the country the world's third largest emitter of CO2, after China and the United States.[14]

Exporting Environmental Degradation and Pollution

India and China are increasingly concerned about the export of pollution and waste to their countries by the United States and the rest of the world. There are loud and frequent popular protests in both countries against factories that source to multinationals and don't observe local water or air quality regulations. In addition, both countries must contend with a serious challenge posed by the trade in electronic waste, which has brought the discarded elec- tronics of the United States and other countries to the poorest communities in their countries. Areas where there is a high con- centration of e-waste recycling have become toxic with dangerous levels of contaminants in the soil and local water supplies.

The United States must clean up its act, while at the same time working to ensure that China and India do not begin to export their waste to other developing countries. Currently, the greater challenge arises from the expansion of Chinese and Indian extrac- tive resource industries. Most important, China is now the largest importer of illegally logged timber in the world; either directly or indirectly, it is furthering the indiscriminate destruction of forests in countries as diverse as Indonesia, Papua New Guinea, Mozambique, and Russia. In some cases, as much as 70 percent of the logs imported from countries by China are illegally cut, contributing not only to the degradation of local environments but also to climate change. Chinese and Indian firms, including Sinopec in Gabon, Shougang in Peru, and Tata in Tanzania, have also come under fire for their poor environmental practices in other extractive industries. As China's and India's economies mature, they may also begin exporting their production and pollution abroad, mirroring the historical practices of much of the advanced industrialized world.

Recommendations and Conclusions: What to Do?

There is no silver bullet. What is needed is nothing short of an Environmental Action Plan for the 21st century that begins by getting our own environmental house in order; pushes us to develop new technologies and the necessary policy environment for the rapid deployment and utilization of these technologies; and works in concert with U.S. NGOs and multinationals as well as other developed economies in Japan and the European Union to approach Asia's environmental challenge in a comprehensive, coordinated and coherent manner.

1. Get our own house in order

Taking action at home to address global climate change, water security, and weak corporate environmental governance is a first step. The United States has little credibility in trying to persuade China and India to do more if we ourselves are not employing best practices. Moreover, U.S. economic competitiveness over the medium and long term will benefit by taking the necessary measures now: enhancing building energy efficiency, adopting a gasoline tax for private automobiles, raising CAFE (Corporate Average Fuel Economy) standards, establishing incentives for expanding the use of renewable energies, and developing a national cap-and-trade system for CO2. Finally, America's global reputation as an environmental leader is at stake. Ensuring that U.S. multinationals adhere to environmental regulations and control the export of electronic waste, or e-waste, is an important first step.

2. Develop and transfer technology

Addressing climate change, water security and improved corporate environmental governance within Asia will hinge to a large extent on access to appropriate technologies. The key challenges for the United States are still market access and protection of intellectual property rights. For the developing countries, the cost of advanced environmental technologies can be prohibitive. There are several steps the United States could take in this regard:

- Provide competitive grants for joint research to result in shared patents among national labs or multinationals in the United States with those in India, China, and other developing Asian countries.

- Press forward with market access and intellectual property rights cases in the World Trade Organization. Begin a process of score-carding regions within China and India based on their environmental performance to encourage multinationals and other investors to do business in those regions with the best environmental records.

- Encourage China and India to increase the level of government expenditure on environmental protection. Both remain far below the level necessary to keep their environmental situations from deteriorating further.

- Continue current efforts by Treasury Secretary Paulsen to develop a global clean energy fund. In addition, the United States could consider a bilateral fund to promote U.S. technology transfer at below market costs. However, any such transfer would have to be contingent on the establishment of the appropriate policy environment in the recipient country.

3. Establish the proper policy environment

Technologies will succeed only if the proper policy environment is in place. The fundamentals of effective environmental protection — including price signals, enforcement capacity, transparency, and the rule of law — are all poorly institutionalized in both China and India. The United States should expend significant effort on capacity building in both countries, including training not only of government officials but also of business and NGO leaders, along with environmental lawyers and judges. An integrated approach that engages the energy, public health, and urban planning arenas, among others, will help ensure the most effective and coordinated adoption of innovative policy efforts and technologies. To accomplish this integration, the United States should consider the following approaches:

- Continue the Strategic Economic Dialogue (SED) under the auspices of the Treasury Department. The SED provides a forum for the United States and China to develop a long-term strategy for cooperation on the environment and energy.

- Strengthen the SED with India and explore the establishment of an SED with Indonesia. A U.S.-Indonesia SED could be particularly important for articulating a vision for forest conservation and compensation in the context of a new global climate framework.

- Initiate an experimental low carbon zone: Qinghua University professor Hu Angang has proposed an experimental low carbon zone in China that would make maximum use of best energy practices. Such an experimental zone might also incorporate water management and other environmental issues.

- Develop twinning projects: Princeton Professor Rob Socolow and others have suggested twinning: marrying provinces in China or states in India with states in the U.S. to promote simultaneous adoption of technologies or policy approaches. Such projects already occur informally; but a far more strategic effort, engaging the wealthiest regions first, would not only advance environmental protection but would also help strengthen broader relations among the countries.

- Engage the corporate sector: Multinationals have an important role to play as well. With U.S. retailers and manufacturers sourcing from hundreds of thousands of factories in China and India, these companies are well positioned to ensure that these factories meet if not exceed the countries' environmental laws and regulations or lose their contracts. Ending the export of electronic waste should also be a top priority.

4. Don't duplicate

The European Union and Japan already have very active collaboration efforts with Asia, and particularly with China, on many areas of energy efficiency and environmental protection. Japan could be an especially significant partner for the developing countries of Asia as a model of industrial energy efficiency. In addition, much of the forward-thinking policy and technology development on issues related to environmental protection in Asia is produced by U.S. NGOs and multinationals. As a result, the next U.S. administration should:

- Take advantage of pre-existing international organizations such as the Organisation for Economic Co-operation and Development (OECD) and the G-8 to think strategically about how best to engage Asia on key areas of common environmental concern.

- Develop a regular consultative framework with U.S. NGOs and multinationals to feed ideas and opportunities regarding cooperation with China and other Asian countries on water security, climate change, and environmental governance into bilateral forums such as the Strategic Economic Dialogue.

---

[1] This statistic refers specifically to the pollutant PM10, the number of cities may be higher or lower depending on the type of air pollutant.

[2] "Beyond Scarcity: Power, Poverty and the Global Water Crisis," Human Development Report 2006, United Nations Development Programme: p.33.

[3] Overall, irrigated agriculture accounts for nearly 79% of water use, industrial use accounts for 13%, and household use 8%. While the relative share of agriculture's water demand is decreasing as industry and household demand grow, in absolute terms, the demand for

water for agriculture is increasing and is unlikely to diminish in the foreseeable future. The sources are several-fold. More affluent Asians use water-consuming appliances and eat more protein, such as meat, which requires more water than grain. Energy is also an important driver of Asia's water landscape. Large-scale generation of electricity invariably requires water, and traditional energy sources such as hydropower and coal are being joined by new, water-intensive fuel opportunities such as biofuels. India and China have both set ambitious goals for biofuel production to limit their growing fossil fuel imports. By 2020, China wants to increase its biofuel production 400% to meet about 9% of its projected gasoline demand. To meet their biofuel targets, an International Water Management Institute report concludes that China would need to produce 26% more maize and India 16% more sugarcane. To produce a liter of maize-based ethanol requires six times more irrigation water than in the United States and more than 25 times as much as in Brazil.

[4] Human Development Report 2006, op. cit., p.142-143.

[5] Asian Water Development Outlook 2007, Asian Development Bank: p.21-22.

[6] Asian Water Development Outlook 2007, op. cit., p.14.

[7] "Beyond Scarcity: Power, Poverty and the Global Water Crisis," Human Development Report 2006 United Nations Development Programme.

[8] "Millions Face Water Shortage in North China, Officials Warn," New York Times (June 6, 2003).

[9] For a more extensive treatment of water security in Asia, see Elizabeth Economy, "Water Security in Asia," forthcoming in Ashley Tellis, ed., Strategic Asia 2008-2009, The National Bureau of Asian Research.

[10] Brahma Chellaney. "Climate Change and Security in Southern Asia: Understanding the National Security Implications," RUSI Journal (April 2007): p.63.

[11] Siddhartha Kumar. "India's Energy Dilemma: coal-powered growth vs climatic disaster," Monsters and Critics online news. http://www.monstersandcritics.com/news/energy-watch/features/article/_1296676.php/Indias_energy_dilemma_Coal-powered_growth_vs_climatic_disaster

[12] "Climate Change and its possible impact on India," Greenpeace. www.greenpeace.org/india/campaigns/choose-positive-energy/what-is-climate-change/climate-change-its-possible

[13] China relies on coal for 70% of its energy and is adding one new coal-fired power plant

every 7-10 days. Industries in China and India are 3-7 times less efficient than those in the developed world and automobile use is increasing dramatically. By 2030, China will likely have more cars on its roads than the United States. India, in turn, forecasts a dramatic expansion in its automobile sector with the delivery of a Tata car that will retail for under US$2000. Urbanization poses an additional threat to managing energy use. Urban residents in China use 3.5 times more energy than their rural counterparts, as a result of poor building energy efficiency and energy-guzzling appliances.

[14] Kumar, op. cit.

REDUCE, MAINTAIN, ENHANCE: U.S. FORCE STRUCTURE CHANGES IN THE ASIA-PACIFIC REGION

Derek J. Mitchell

Issue: What are the military/security challenges in East Asia that a new U.S. administration should focus on? Is the U.S. force posture in the Western Pacific appropriate for the protection of U.S. interests and those of its allies and friends? In the view of some observers, U.S. capabilities for power projection in East Asia remain strong but the political underpinnings for such use of power have weakened. To what extent is the U.S. forward presence viewed by Asians as contributing to regional stability or as increasing the risks of military confrontations?

Introduction

For decades, it has been axiomatic among American and most East Asian strategists that the U.S. military presence in East Asia has served an essential role in preserving regional stability by maintaining a benign balance of power in the region. According to this view, the U.S. presence has served as a buffer and has perhaps deterred conflict in a region still fraught with latent tensions and unresolved disputes left over from history. In the process, with the U.S. acting as security guarantor, regional states have been able to channel their resources into confidence-building and internal development rather than arms races and competing blocs.

During the Cold War, the U.S. military presence in Asia was vital to the global campaign to contain the spread of communism and it served to reassure regional states that Japanese militarization and aggression were things of the past. With the fall of the Soviet Union and ideological moderation in China, some questioned the rationale for continuing Cold War-era alliances and military presence in the region, particularly given the "peace dividend" of the 1990s and uncertainty about exactly what threat required such continued investment of U.S. resources.

Both the Bill Clinton and George W. Bush administrations determined, however, that residual problems from the Cold War continued to exist in East Asia, requiring continued U.S. attention and commitment. They also recognized the growing strategic importance of East Asia due to the region's tremendous economic development. At the same time, most regional nations continued to welcome the U.S. military presence as a benign factor whose military presence offered reassurance and stability during a time of great political and economic transition.

A new U.S. administration will need to assess for itself the key challenges to U.S. interests in East Asia in the coming years, and determine whether the U.S. military is configured and positioned correctly to protect these interests.

Security Challenges in East Asia

The dynamism and diversity of East Asia create not only tremendous opportunities, but also challenges for international stability and security. While vehicles for confidence-building and dialogue have proliferated to deal with past and present differences, and the prospect of armed conflict between states appears small, the region still contains two of the world's most dangerous flashpoints: the Taiwan Strait impasse and continued division of the Korean Peninsula. North Korea's nuclear program and missile development will remain a source of instability in Northeast Asia — and potentially for the nonproliferation regime as a whole — for years to come. While the return of the Kuomintang Party (KMT) to power in Taiwan appears to enhance the prospect for stability across the Taiwan Strait, careful U.S. attention to cross-Strait affairs remains essential to prevent miscalculation or provocation by one side or the other from raising tensions and threatening regional stability. The next U.S. administration — like all administrations over the past 50 years — must continue to give priority attention to both of these situations, as each could drag the United States into military conflict at a moment's notice given its longstanding commitments to the security of both South Korea and Taiwan, and to regional stability more broadly.

The rise of China as a political, economic, and military power will also require close observation. China is party to several lingering territorial disputes: in the East China Sea (with Japan), South China Sea (with several Southeast Asian nations), along its border with India, and even with Korea. While there is no reason to assume that China's emergence will inevitably prove hostile to regional stability and security, uncertainty about the trajectory and intentions underlying China's rise may pose a substantial challenge to the regional system and established order. Indeed, the rise of such a huge power in both economic and military terms could lead to pressures on regional states to either balance against or bandwagon with China — or to hedge their bets as they carefully gauge changes in the regional power balance over time.

So-called "non-traditional" security challenges are also emerging to become as important to the region as traditional state threats.

These challenges include environmental degradation, humanitarian crises, disaster relief, energy security, human and drug trafficking, and health/infectious diseases. To the degree that the United States is viewed as helpful and in fact capable of addressing these real and immediate regional concerns in a timely fashion, it will continue to burnish its credentials as an essential component of stability and security in arenas that are relevant to East Asia. Indeed, the rapid U.S. response, in partnership with its allies, to the humanitarian crisis following the 2004 tsunami; the unrealized potential of its offer of assistance to Burma (also known as Myanmar) following the May 2008 cyclone; and its previous success in suppressing wildfires in Indonesia among other natural disasters, demonstrated the unique contributions U.S. military forces continue to offer the region aside from the obvious deterrent capabilities of its hard power.

Maritime security is another critical common interest given that a third of world trade and half of the world's oil pass through the region's sea lanes. The ability to ensure free passage through these sea lanes is an essential component of U.S. regional military engagement, and has profound effects on regional — and indeed global — security.

Finally, although the Bush administration was faulted for its single-minded focus on the threat from radical jihadists around the world, including in its approach to Southeast Asia; the presence of Islamic extremist groups in the region with a track record of terrorism and connections to al-Qaeda does merit attention from the United States as a continued and valid security concern.

U.S. Force Presence

In the aftermath of the Cold War, U.S. force presence in East Asia underwent adjustments to address new strategic conditions and capabilities. U.S. forces have remained stationed in Japan and South Korea — although the number of personnel has steadily declined, and bases have been consolidated and repositioned in recent years. At the same time, the Pentagon has steadily increased its deployments on U.S. territory in the Asia-Pacific region. The United States has boosted its maritime expeditionary and long-range (air) strike capability through increased deployments in Alaska and Hawaii. The 2001 and 2006 Quadrennial Defense Review called for increased naval presence in the Western Pacific and more home-porting of surface and subsurface combatants, including potential home-porting of an additional aircraft carrier in theater to the one at Yokosuka. Guam has become a preferred forward location for sustained presence, and to increase deterrence and rapid response capabilities to deal with challenges over a great distance in the Asia–Pacific region and beyond.

Within Asia, the United States has sought to combine the use of large, permanent bases in Japan and South Korea with other non-permanent strategically located sites elsewhere to enable a kind of "lily pad" strategy in which U.S. forces may move with agility and regularity among different access points around Asia and the globe. In this way, the United States may maintain an effective and efficient power projection capability to address unforeseen challenges, while leaving behind a relatively unobtrusive footprint.

Indeed, growing resentment within Japanese and Korean communities about the inconvenience and dangers of living around U.S. military bases have resulted in increasing constraints on U.S. exercise, training, and operations. Pentagon planners have therefore sought to move forces to places where they may operate and train flexibly and relatively unconstrained, and where the United States could be more confident that it could sustain its presence over the longer term. Simultaneously, they have maintained an ability to surge forces back into Japan and Korea quickly when needed, to ensure that traditional deterrence dynamics can be upheld.

The advent of lighter, faster, more mobile, and more lethal power projection capabilities that can be deployed and networked over great distances — what the Bush administration called "transformation" and the Clinton administration termed the "revolution in military affairs" — also enabled U.S. planners to consider changes in U.S. force structure in East Asia. At the same time, the Bush administration sought to economize in its commitments by turning over more defense burdens to its allies, so that Washington might focus on more complex challenges of maintaining peace and stability in East Asia and around the world.

Recommendations and Conclusions

The reduction in forward deployed forces in East Asia — as opposed to the broader "Asia-Pacific" region — raised questions in some Asian circles as to whether the U.S. commitment as regional security guarantor was receding, particularly as the United States became distracted by wars in Iraq and Afghanistan and other aspects of the "global war on terrorism." The Bush administration sought to do away with the notion that numbers of troops deployed in the region — "approximately 100,000" in 1990s parlance — reflected U.S. commitment, and argued that "capabilities" were a better measure.

The region nonetheless remained wary of what the reductions signaled about U.S. commitment over the long-term. Others alternatively noted with concern that pulling back forces from East Asia to Guam, etc., could allow the United States to take unilateral provocative action in the region with less risk, shielded by distance and leaving allies on the front lines.

The logic of affirming "real" capabilities over symbolic numbers as a measure of commitment has a strong foundation as long as U.S. commitment and capabilities are evident in tangible ways and sustainable over time. To this end, the United States should continually demonstrate its presence through exercises, trainings, and rapid response deployments to the region to reaffirm U.S. reliability and capabilities. Given the unwelcome intrusiveness of long-term deployments on land, the United States should put more emphasis on sea-borne demonstrations of presence, while retaining access points on land as necessary. When based or deployed on shore, the United States should also seek to increasingly co-locate its forces with those of the host nation to promote greater operational synergy, share operational burdens, and ensure that U.S. forces are viewed as guests rather than occupiers on foreign soil.

The United States should continually demonstrate its presence through exercises, trainings, and rapid response deployments to the region to reaffirm U.S. reliability and capabilities.

In the process, the United States must continuously engage its regional allies and friends about their perspectives on prospective changes in U.S. force structure and their impact on regional power balances. Close consultation will be essential to manage the paradoxical desire among Asian states to both retain U.S. regional "presence," and reduce the overall U.S. military footprint on their own soil.

Close consultation will be essential to manage the paradoxical desire among Asian states to both retain U.S. regional "presence," and reduce the overall U.S. military footprint on their own soil.

At the same time, the United States should continue to press its allies to step up with their own contributions to regional security to supplement U.S. traditional commitments. The United States will increasingly need its partners to share the burden and to build confidence with other militaries, including China, to create a stable and secure region. The notion of a "1000-ship Navy" that seeks to combine assets of many nations to promote a secure maritime commons should continue to be developed.

While the overall force restructure plans put forward by the Bush administration are reasonable, the primary challenge in coming years will be implementation. Changes on the Korean peninsula seem to be on track, if slightly behind schedule. Uncertainty over political will in Tokyo to fund prospective moves remains an obstacle that will need consistent attention in coming years. Elsewhere in Asia, the U.S. "lily pad" strategy of replacing permanent bases with access points will also face challenges as the United States seeks to identify new "cooperative security locations" in coming years.

A new U.S. administration in 2009 will likely revisit the Bush administration's realignment plans around the world, including in East Asia. But the essential focus on capabilities over numbers, and more flexible, mobile forces that reduce the burden on local communities, likely will not — and indeed should not — change.

After initial doubts, the region seems to have come to accept the U.S. military strategy to "reduce (numbers), maintain (presence), and enhance (capabilities)" as generally acceptable and benign to regional stability. A new U.S. administration in 2009 will likely revisit the Bush administration's realignment plans around the world, including in East Asia. But the essential focus on capabilities over numbers, and more flexible, mobile forces that reduce the burden on local communities, likely will not — and indeed should not — change.

ALLIANCE RELATIONSHIPS

Michael McDevitt

Issue: Asia is in a transition phase where countries are disinclined to adopt threat-based approaches to enhancing security, preferring cooperative measures. All U.S. allies in Asia attach importance to keeping their relations with China on an even keel. Under these circumstances, does the United States need to rethink its conceptual approach to regional security? Are there ways the United States can transform and revitalize its alliance relationships in ways that would retain and enhance their relevance in dealing with potential problems while keeping in step with shifts in regional attitudes? Are there other steps the United States should take that would strengthen perceptions on the part of East Asian countries that the United States was properly engaged in the region and that its continuing presence enhanced security in the Western Pacific?

Introduction

The issue this essay will address is whether the United States needs to rethink its conceptual approach to regional security. This is an important question since there is a perception that Asia may be in the midst of rethinking its approach to security — away from so-called "threat based" security frameworks to a more cooperative approach. Whether or not this generalization is accurate — if you queried leaders in Tokyo, Seoul, Taipei, Singapore, and New Delhi who believe they face real threats, it is probably not — it nonetheless raises the issue of how America's alliance-based security architecture can evolve and adapt to the very real trend of Asian community-building. The reality is that cooperative security approaches and bilateral alliances are not mutually exclusive. They can, and should, co-exist.

Cooperative security is the only sensible way to address transnational security problems because solving these problems requires cooperation among many states. At the same time, security-based alliances and strategic partnerships remain the best way to deter aggression, reassure friends, and maintain the credible balance of power that is necessary for regional stability.

The next administration is going to be faced with the need to reassure Asian countries that Washington is not so fixated on the Middle East that it will neglect its interests in Asia. It will need to persuade leaders across the region that America intends to remain a force for stability and enhanced regional security in East Asia for the foreseeable future. And, at the same it must take advantage of the growing regional momentum toward cooperative security in a way that will reconcile today's security architecture with the cooperative approach that most Asian nations favor.

Washington must take advantage of the growing regional momentum toward cooperative security in a way that will reconcile today's security architecture with the cooperative approach that most Asian nations favor.

Alliance-Based Security Architecture Has Worked Well

For almost 50 years, Asia's security environment has been stable and relatively predictable. After the 1953 armistice that ended combat in Korea, Asia's security environment quickly settled into a unique balance of power, in which the continental powers of the Soviet Union and the People's Republic of China were "balanced" by the U.S.-led coalition of the Asian littoral powers of Japan, the Republic of Korea, the Republic of China, and for a while, the multi-national Southeast Asia Treaty Organization (SEATO).

There are a number of reasons why stability persisted, but arguably the most important one is that a real military balance existed.[1] The military capability of each side was able to "trump" any attempt by the other side to intrude in a militarily significant way into its domain. The USSR and the PRC were safe from invasion, thanks to their large armies, vast territories and nuclear weapons. Japan and Taiwan were safe from invasion and maritime blockade thanks to U.S. air and sea power that alliances made possible. While Southeast Asia had to struggle with Communist insurgencies – and Vietnam, Laos, and Cambodia were "lost" – the strategic balance did not change appreciably. In the meantime, non-communist Southeast Asia, including U.S. alliance partners Thailand and the Philippines, prospered and gradually democratized.

In a very real sense, Washington's current security architecture is, as Beijing frequently reminds us, an artifact of the Cold War (Beijing frequently refers to the network of bilateral alliances put in place in the 1950s as a "relic"). In truth however, the alliance system has proven supple enough to evolve and adapt, mainly because the alliances are defensive in character and are therefore "reactive" to the evolving security environment. In Europe, the

North Atlantic Treaty Organization (NATO) is a classic example of how a defensive alliance adapts to the changing nature of the security environment.

Historic Perspective

Since the U.S. annexation of the Philippines, Washington has tried to keep the Asian region from being dominated by a hostile or anti-American power. A century ago, American strategists faced a serious security problem: How to protect sovereign U.S. territory remote from the U.S. mainland and literally in the backyard of Japan, a rising Asian power.

Between 1905 and 1941, Washington tried a variety of approaches to safeguarding U.S. interests in East Asia. Efforts to bandwagon with Japan were followed by attempts to shape Japanese behavior through the combination of naval arms limitation agreements and multilateral security guarantees at the Washington Conference of 1920-21. As it turned out, Japan refused to be "shaped," and belated U.S. attempts to arrest Japanese expansion through economic sanctions and the posturing of the main U.S. fleet "forward" in Pearl Harbor as a deterrent also failed to alter Japanese behavior. If there was a lesson from the first half of the 20th century for Cold War strategists, it seems to have been: Do not fall behind in a military capability competition with a new Asian power.

The 21st Century and East Asian Geo-Strategic Circumstances — Back to the Future?

Today, the pivotal question for today's policymakers in Washington — and in the Asian region — is whether China's growing military capabilities are recreating the same security problem that strategists faced in 1905 and 1953. Looking back 100 years ago in East Asia when the United States worried about Japan, or 58 years ago in Europe when it worried about the Soviet Union, it seems that America's strategic circumstances vis-à-vis East Asia have changed the least — only the names of friends and potential security problems have changed. Although the relationships between China, Japan, Russia, Korea, and Taiwan have flip-flopped several times; the United States still faces the geographically imposed reality of how best to protect its vital interests and meet defense obligations in areas that are remote from its homeland, and in the "backyard" of a rapidly modernizing Asian military power — China.

Looking back 100 years ago in East Asia when the United States worried about Japan, or 58 years ago in Europe when it worried about the Soviet Union, it seems that America's strategic circumstances vis-à-vis East Asia have changed the least — only the names of friends and potential security problems have changed.

Modernizing China: Changing the Strategic Balance

China is improving its military capabilities for off-shore operations, albeit largely for defensive purposes. However, as its military capabilities improve by fielding weapons systems that can protect its maritime approaches, China is entering the maritime sphere traditionally overseen by the United States and its allies for over 50 years. This is beginning to upset the balance of power between continental and maritime powers that has been so successful in preserving stability in the region. Specifically, China is developing a credible ability to deny access to U.S. forces by knitting together broad ocean surveillance systems, a large number of submarines, land-based aircraft with cruise missiles, and ballistic missile systems that can target ships on the high seas.

The U.S. strategic position in the Asian littoral depends on its ability to use the region's seas to guarantee its East Asian allies' security and pursue American national interests. Beijing's central wartime goal in securing its maritime frontier is to keep U.S. power at arms length, and to render the U.S. unable to intervene militarily. This could constrain U.S. access to the region which in turn worsens the security environment for Japan, Taiwan, and potentially, South Korea.

Beijing's central wartime goal in securing its maritime frontier is to keep U.S. power at arms length, and to render the U.S. unable to intervene militarily. This could constrain U.S. access to the region which in turn worsens the security environment for Japan, Taiwan, and potentially, South Korea.

Defensive Alliances Essential for Sustaining U.S. Military Influence in the Region

As China slowly alters the Western Pacific's strategic balance, the United States naval and air forces are 50 to 60 percent fewer than they were at the end of the Cold War. This greatly reduces U.S. flexibility in maintaining a strong overseas presence capable of honoring defense commitments and providing regional stability. Sending forces on routine six- or eight-month rotations is not sustainable over the long term; forces need to be permanent and on bases in East Asia. Without fixed facilities available in Japan and South Korea, sustaining today's level of American military capability in East Asia will not be possible.

Since 2003, the Bush administration has attempted to "transform" the U.S. military posture in the Western Pacific and East Asia to better position it for the future. In Japan and Korea, this involves significant redeployment of U.S. ground forces and actions to reduce frictions associated with the close intermingling of U.S. bases and local populaces. Part of this transformation includes transferring more U.S. forces to the U.S. Territory of Guam. Guam is also being used to introduce additional U.S. capabilities, such as submarines and routine bomber deployments, to the Asia-Pacific region in order to maintain America's current advantages in the face of growing Chinese maritime power.

In Southeast Asia, Washington has designated the Philippines and Thailand as major non-NATO allies and has paid consider-able attention to strengthening its defense relationship with Singapore. Since 9/11, transnational threats such as terrorism in Southeast Asia have been the most urgent. Although Washington sees its counter-terrorism cooperation with Southeast Asian nations as being quite successful, Southeast Asia's security concerns include not only terrorism, but illegal migration, piracy, environmental degradation, and trafficking in weapons, drugs, and people. Southeast Asian governments correctly believe that cooperative security approaches are the only way to address these complex issues.

When it comes to Southeast Asia, the U.S.'s closest relationships are with Australia and Singapore. In Australia, the recently elected Rudd government has publicly acknowledged that the Australia-New Zealand-U.S. (ANZUS) security alliance remains central to its security. While the United States' security relationship with Singapore is embodied in the Framework Agreement for Strategic Cooperation rather than a formal alliance treaty, Singapore is for all practical purposes an ally, and since the early 1990s has been America's closest ASEAN (Association of Southeast Asian Nations) partner. Washington must treat Singapore's specific observations regarding the emerging Southeast Asian multi-layered security architecture seriously — this will be an important issue for the next U.S. administration.

America's alliance structure with India has seen a dramatic change in the past decade. U.S. attitudes toward India have changed from perceiving the country as a "problem" for Washington because of its nuclear weapons tests to viewing it as a "strategic partner." From India's perspective, reaching a security understanding with Washington makes sense, as it lives in a very dangerous neighborhood. This also means, however, that India's security focus is close to home.

The U.S.-India strategic partnership is the most current example of the continued relevancy of bilateral defense understandings as an important policy tool in advancing the interests of both partners. Whereas collective measures are the appropriate diplomatic tool for transnational issues, bilateralism in security matters related to other nation states still resonates throughout Asia.

Bilateral security relationships between the United States and Asian countries will endure as long as North Korea, China, a resurgent Russia, or other regional threats convince partner countries that a relationship with the United States is the best way to ensure their security. The predictability of a security relationship with Washington is much more appealing than relying on any unproven multinational institution — especially ones without guarantees of a military response to aggression. (The multilateral security treaties signed at the 1920-21 Washington Conference failed because the signatories' only obligation in response to aggression was "to consult.") On Washington's part, as long the United States believes it is in its interests to maintain a credible military presence in the region, it will sustain its many defense obligations throughout the Asia-Pacific.

Introducing Cooperative Security Relationships into Asia's Security Architecture

New thinking about multilateralism and cooperative security in East Asia has been led by Southeast Asian nations and ASEAN. For more than 10 years, the United States has worked to transform and strengthen its bilateral relationships. Simultaneously, ASEAN and, more recently, China have been creating Asian institutions focused on dialogue and relationship building.

This regional trend is specifically addressed by Catharin Dalpino's essay in this volume and – aside from one comment – will not be further explored in this essay. In 2007, the Beijing-promoted East Asia Summit (EAS) was created as the only Asian regional forum with the mandate to discuss Asian security and political issues at the summit level – minus the United States. Given America's central role in Asia-Pacific security, it is strategically absurd for the United States not to have a place at the table when these issues are addressed.

One may ask why cooperative security concepts have taken root in Southeast Asia rather than Northeast Asia, where security problems associated with China and Taiwan and North Korea have long been much more immediate and dangerous. The answer stems from the nature of the security problem. Transnational, non-traditional security issues vary greatly from traditional power-based security issues, as the emphasis is on common challenges and the need to collectively find common solutions. Like traditional security issues, transnational security issues often require military instruments. The "peacetime use of military capability" is something the U.S. has done for decades. An example is the annual CARAT (cooperation afloat readiness and training) exercises by the U.S. and Southeast Asian navies aimed at improving the capacity of partner navies to deal with the transnational issues of terrorism and illegal trafficking.

In Northeast Asia, however, continued reliance on formal security alliances as the instruments of choice is directly related to the type of security challenge faced by each U.S. partner — be it Japan, South Korea, or Taiwan. The challenges presented to these partners are country specific, are unique in terms of geography, involve issues of sovereignty, and share no common canonical enemy. They are most sensibly addressed by bilateral alliances.

However, over the last decade or so, factors have emerged which suggest that cooperative security in Northeast Asia may be coming into its own. The economic integration of this sub-region — with

China as the hub of a network of relations because of its economic "open door" — has gone on despite periods of tension between the countries of the region. Other aspects of globalization, such as the spread of popular culture, regional tourism, and communications, have created a new atmosphere of sub-regionalism where the economic, communications, social, travel, and cultural linkages among the nations make a region-wide security structure seem plausible. Addressing shared interests such as energy security, sea lane security, and air pollution reduction through such a regional security structure is desirable.

The obvious vehicle to developing a sub-regional cooperative security framework is the six-party process, which was put in place in 2002 by the Bush administration to address the North Korea nuclear weapons program. Since then, there has been a great deal of speculation over the eventual transformation of this issue-specific dialogue into a more permanent regional one. So far, Washington has indicated receptivity to this idea, but has properly kept the focus on North Korea.

The resolution of the North Korean nuclear problem may take some time. Therefore, a return to trilateralism — between U.S.-Japan-China and U.S.-Japan-South Korea — may provide a better way to begin cooperating on issues beyond North Korea. This is not hard to imagine as the precedent of a U.S.-Japan-ROK dialogue is already set and the U.S.-Japan-Australia dialogue suggests a practical template for such a process. A network of trilateral dialogues as a starting point for regional cooperation may be a better building-block for Northeast Asian cooperative security.

Recommendations and Conclusions

As long as China looms large in the security calculations of all of
its Asian neighbors, it is unlikely that there will be any organized
regional push back of the U.S. alliance architecture. Maintaining a
balance of power is central to strategic calculations regarding East
Asia, and the United States is the only possible hedge against a
militarily assertive China. Washington must ensure that the region
perceives U.S. military capability as viable in the face of China's
military improvements, while avoiding the perception that the
United States is trying to contain China.

Washington must ensure that the region perceives U.S. military

capability as viable in the face of China's military improvements,

while avoiding the perception that the United States is trying to

contain China.

A new U.S. administration must also decide if *ad hoc* multilaterial-
ism — for example, "coalitions of the willing" — makes sense for
the future. East Asians are definitely inching toward institutionalized multilateralism and there is no reason for America not to
embrace it as we have in Europe. Making membership in the
EAS a central political objective is a sensible step to take. It will
not undermine U.S. bilateral alliances – and the best way to shape
outcomes that support U.S. interests is to be part of the process.
Becoming a part of the EAS and other Asian multilateral organizations would balance our political and military influence in East

Asia — combining an alliance-based security presence and a multi-lateral-based political presence.

For Washington to become a credible player in a multilateral security framework it must embrace the fundamental premise of cooperative security in Asia: dialogue. The Asian concept is that dialogue results in understanding and leads to practical cooperation aimed at solving problems. Washington has long been impatient with so-called Asian talk shops that are short on action. The fact is however, over the years the Asian "dialogue approach" has helped to maintain peace in Southeast Asia and has resulted in various modest cooperative measures that address non-traditional security issues such as piracy. If Washington is not willing to embrace this style of security-related diplomacy, it risks being left out of cooperative security institutions and seeing its influence attenuated by China – who has forthrightly embraced it.

---

[1] During much of this period China was preoccupied by the internal turmoil of the Great Leap Forward and Cultural Revolution, and support of "revolutionary" movements in Southeast Asia. The Soviet Union was decidedly Eurocentric in its focus, and its out-of-area military operations centered on small-scale deployments to bases in Vietnam.

CHINA POLICY FOR THE NEXT U.S. ADMINISTRATION

Harry Harding

Issue: Should the United States fundamentally alter its policy toward Beijing, given American concerns about China's international behavior, its dissatisfaction with bilateral economic relations, and its dissatisfaction with the domestic political and economic situation in China? If so, in what direction? And if not, can present policy be implemented more effectively?

Introduction

Ever since the normalization of diplomatic relations with Beijing at the end of 1978, American policy toward China has comprised four major themes.

First, a policy governing our relationship with Taiwan, often called our *"one China policy."* Under it, Washington maintains diplomatic relations only with Beijing, but has created a non-governmental organization to represent its interests in Taipei. The United States has also declared that it would welcome any final definition of Taiwan's relationship with the mainland that occurred peacefully and with mutual consent of both parties, but would oppose any attempt by either side to impose its will unilaterally on the other.

Second, a policy of *comprehensive engagement* with China, using frequent high-level official dialogue — including periodic summit meetings — to advance the two countries' complementary economic and security interests while resolving or managing their differences over specific bilateral, regional, and global issues.

Third, a policy of encouraging China's *integration* into the international community. Over time, the United States has helped secure Beijing's membership in such key institutions as the World Bank, the International Monetary Fund (IMF), and the World Trade Organization (WTO). More generally, it has supported China's integration into the global economy, and encouraged Beijing to accept international norms regarding domestic governance and international conduct.

Fourth, a policy of *reassuring* China that the United States wishes it well. Washington has periodically declared its interest in a "secure," "strong," "confident," "prosperous," and "stable" China. In 1997-98, the Clinton administration agreed with Beijing on the goal of "building toward a constructive strategic partnership" for the 21st century.

Since 1978, the American presidential election cycle has occasioned episodic debate about the wisdom of this mainstream policy toward China. In 1980, Ronald Reagan criticized the impact of the normalization of U.S.-China relations on Taiwan, calling for the reestablishment of some kind of official relationship with Taipei. In 1992, in the aftermath of the Tiananmen Crisis of 1989, Bill Clinton promised to condition the then-annual renewal of China's most-favored-nation (MFN) trading status on an improvement in its human rights record, suggesting that the United States wanted China not just to be secure and prosperous, but democratic as well. In 2000, George W. Bush criticized the Clinton administration for regarding China as a potential "strategic partner" of the United States, describing it instead as a "strategic competitor." Now, in

2008, several candidates for the presidency have called for a tougher American trade policy toward China, charging Beijing with unfair trade practices that restrict U.S. exports to China and produce a large and growing trade imbalance between the two countries.

But even when candidates critical of American policy toward China have entered the White House, the changes they promised during their election campaigns have been short-lived. Before his inauguration in 1981, President Reagan stopped calling for the reestablishment of official relations with Taiwan, and by August 1982, had agreed to limit American arms sales to the island. In 1994, President Clinton backed away from his threat to terminate China's MFN status, even while acknowledging that Beijing's human rights record had not significantly improved. And within a few months after his inauguration in 2001, President George W. Bush stopped calling China a "strategic competitor" and once again described the U.S.-China relationship as "constructive" and "cooperative." Once in office, presidents who were originally critics of the mainstream policy have come to appreciate the wisdom of maintaining it.

Once in office, presidents who were originally critics of the mainstream policy have come to appreciate the wisdom of maintaining it.

Although the current Bush administration has, like its predecessors, abandoned the idea of a radical departure from mainstream China policy, it has redefined that policy in subtle but significant ways:

- The "one-China policy" has been adjusted to become more supportive of Taiwan's security needs and its desire for a greater role in international affairs, while also more explicit in opposing any unilateral declaration of independence. The United States has been more willing to sell advanced weapons to Taipei and to upgrade its military-to-military links with the island. Although still refusing to acknowledge that Taiwan is an independent sovereign state, and while still opposing its entrance into international organizations where membership is restricted to such states, Washington has sought other ways of expanding Taiwan's participation in the international community.

- Integration has been supplemented by the proposition that, having joined virtually all relevant international regimes and organizations, it is time for China to become a "responsible stakeholder" in the international system. The United States wants China to do more — through rhetorical pressure, diplomatic initiatives, and economic and military sanctions — to enforce international norms and to implement the decisions of the international organizations it has joined.

- Engagement has been complemented by a strategy of "hedging": while trying to cooperate with China to manage differences and advance common interests, the United States also insures against the possibility that this policy might not succeed. Hedging has involved plans to relocate and strengthen the American forces deployed in the Western Pacific; reinvigorate American alliances in the region; and build more extensive political and security ties with important non-allied states such as Singapore, Indonesia, and India. This gives Washington the ability to resist Chinese initiatives that it might find objectionable.

The Alternatives

Revising the mainstream policy in this way has strengthened its political base in the United States. But it has not ended all debate. There is still much frustration in Congress and the general public with China – and with American policy toward China. Beijing has disappointed those who expected 30 years of substantial economic reform and rapid economic growth to produce Western-style democracy. China's bilateral trade surplus has led to charges that, despite its membership in the WTO, Beijing still engages in a variety of unfair trading practices. And even if China shares some key American objectives, particularly the promotion of promoting prosperity and stability in Asia and the prevention of the spread of weapons of mass destruction, the two countries often differ over concrete measures to promote those goals.

While the critics' frustrations with China's behavior at home and abroad are understandable, their proposals for a fundamental change of policy are either infeasible or counterproductive.

These frustrations have become evident during the 2008 elections. Some critics have proposed unilateral economic sanctions against China, such as imposing punitive tariffs on Chinese goods or even withdrawing Beijing's MFN trade status to reduce the trade imbalance. Others have suggested replacing the policy of integration with the former policy of containment. Still, others have called for reestablishing diplomatic relations with Taiwan. Some of these proposals, if adopted, would mean abandoning some of the core components of the mainstream China policy that has been in place since the late 1970s.

While the critics' frustrations with China's behavior at home and abroad are understandable, their proposals for a fundamental change of policy are either infeasible or counterproductive. Some of these proposals include:

- Withdrawing Beijing's most-favored-nation status, which would mean the termination of normal commercial relations with China. This would cause great damage to the interests of American exporters and investors who do business there, as well as American consumers who benefit from low-cost imports from China. The imposition of unilateral economic sanctions against Beijing would violate the rules of the WTO, and would risk a trade war with China that would also damage U.S. economic interests.

- Restoring diplomatic relations with Taiwan, which would produce a profound crisis in U.S.-China relations. Given its commitment to the one-China principle — which holds that other countries can recognize either Beijing or Taipei but not both — Beijing would have no choice but to respond by breaking diplomatic relations with the United States. Even more important, Beijing would conclude that the United States had decided to adopt a fundamentally hostile stance toward China. Such a development would not even be welcomed on Taiwan, whose newly elected government is now committed to resuming political dialogue and expanding economic ties with China.

- "Containing" China, which would also be difficult. Unlike the former Soviet Union, China is expanding its influence not by military aggression or subversion, but by expanding commercial relationships, providing development assistance, creating new regional organizations in Central Asia and East Asia, and helping to manage key regional and transnational issues. Most of these initiatives are welcomed by China's partners. Although some countries object to some aspects of Beijing's foreign policy and worry about China's longer-term intentions, their concerns are not great enough to join in a U.S.-led "containment" of China. At present, a policy of hedging against the uncertainties surrounding Beijing's future intentions and capabilities is more suitable than a policy of containment.

Recommendations and Conclusions

In short, the best strategy to take toward China is not to abandon the revised mainstream policy, but rather to implement it more effectively. How might this be done?

- Washington should continue to engage China in frequent, high-level discussions, in both bilateral and multilateral forums; but with a vastly expanded agenda that includes counter-proliferation, regional stability, Third World development, and global prosperity. China and the United States share common interests in these issues, and China increasingly has the resources to contribute effectively to their solution. Increasingly, this will require bargaining: making accommodations to China in exchange for Chinese accommodations to our interests, or compromising on best how to advance common objectives.

- The U.S. should build deeper linkages with friends and

allies so that we can cooperate, when necessary, in challenging Chinese initiatives that we find objectionable. This is
not best done through the creation of a formal "concert of
democracies." Defining the membership of such a grouping
will be difficult in Asia, and many prospective members will
be reluctant to participate in anything that appears to
involve the containment of China. Instead, this strategy is
better pursued through an omni-directional diplomacy that
maximizes the number of potential partners that might join
ad hoc coalitions to counter specific Chinese policies to
which they object.

The best strategy to take toward China is not to abandon

the revised mainstream policy, but rather to implement it

more effectively.

- We should also continue to undertake the prudent strengthening of American forces in the Western Pacific, but reassure
China that we do not seek, or even expect, an implacably
confrontational or even competitive strategic relationship.
Beijing says that its military acquisitions and deployments
are a reasonable response to legitimate security concerns,
including the use of military capabilities for peacekeeping
and humanitarian purposes. We should say the same about
our own.

- The U.S. should support the further integration of China
into the international community, including Beijing's partic-

ipation in the International Energy Agency and the Missile Technology Control Regime. In addition, China should be brought into a new grouping of major economies – either an expanded version of the G-8 or an entirely new organization that includes major emerging markets like China, India, and Brazil. And we should welcome China's participation in creating new institutions and regimes to deal with emerging transnational issues such as energy security, climate change, and transborder investment.

- Washington should encourage China to uphold and enforce the international norms from which it has benefited so significantly. These include the norms against proliferation and against gross violations of human rights, and conditions governing development assistance to Third World governments. To do so, we need to demonstrate that these norms reflect broad international consensus, and not simply the preferences of the United States or other developed economies. We also need to demonstrate to Beijing that promoting international respect for those norms is in China's own interest.

- Finally, we should seek greater Chinese compliance with its obligations under the WTO. Imposing unilateral trade sanctions against China is not in keeping with our preference for a rules-based international trade regime, and would set a bad example for America's other trading partners. The better approach is a more vigorous use of that body's dispute resolution mechanism.

Even when supplemented by hedging and enforcement, engagement and integration are not sufficient. The United States should also adopt broader policies that are necessary in their own right, but are also appropriate strategies for responding to the rise of China. These include efforts to maintain America's economic competitiveness, rebuild public support for an open trading system, restore our international influence, avoid overstretching our military capability, enhance the legitimacy of key global and regional institutions, and ensure stability and prosperity across Asia. In combination, a strong America, effective international institutions, and a robust balance of power will increase the chances that China's rise will remain peaceful and the U.S.-China relationship will remain essentially cooperative.

In combination, a strong America, effective international institutions, and a robust balance of power will increase the chances that China's rise will remain peaceful and the U.S.-China relationship will remain essentially cooperative.

All these are long-term objectives. But what should be the immediate priorities for a new administration? Other than the situation in the Taiwan Strait, as discussed in David Lampton's contribution to this volume, three sets of issues will be particularly important to the near-term future of U.S.-China relations: reducing our differences over trade and investment, working together to secure the denuclearization of the Korean Peninsula, and reaching an agreement to meet the challenge of climate change. Economic issues presently pose the greatest risk of undermining domestic American support for the mainstream China policy, and therefore need to be addressed with some urgency. Denuclearizing the Korean peninsula is important not only for its own sake, but as an example of the benefits that can be achieved from U.S.-China cooperation. The two countries' responses to the problem of climate change will be a key test of their ability to address difficult issues where they agree on goals but differ on solutions.

The two countries' responses to the problem of climate change will be a key test of their ability to address difficult issues where they agree on goals but differ on solutions.

Managing the U.S.-China relationship should be one of the most important objectives for the next administration. As soon as is feasible, the next president should reiterate the American interest in building a positive relationship with China, and reaffirm that there will be continuity in U.S. policy toward China. The new administration should establish and maintain regular high-level dialogues with Chinese leaders — and then vigorously address the core issues of commerce, Korea, and climate.

A MOMENT OF OPPORTUNITY IN THE TAIWAN STRAIT?

David M. Lampton

Issue: How should a new administration manage its relations with Taiwan? Are adjustments needed in the U.S. policy framework for handling Taiwan-related matters? Can the status quo be sustained for an indefinite period and are there steps a new administration can take that would promote a peaceful resolution?

> "These principles of one China and peaceful resolution of the Taiwan question remain the core of our China policy. While our policy has been constant, the situation has not and cannot remain static. We support a continuing evolutionary process toward a peaceful resolution of the Taiwan issue. The pace, however, will be determined by the Chinese on either side of the Taiwan Strait, free of outside pressure.

> "For our part, we have welcomed developments, including indirect trade and increasing human interchange, which have contributed to a relaxation of tensions in the Taiwan Strait. Our steadfast policy seeks to foster an environment in which such developments can continue to take place."

> — *Secretary of State George P. Shultz, March 5, 1987, Shanghai, China. Then-Mayor Jiang Zemin, host.*

The Current Situation: The Possible Opportunity

A new administration assumed office in Taipei in May 2008, while a new administration comes into office in Washington in January 2009. In turn, both new administrations will have a Hu Jintao-Wen Jiabao regime early in its second term to deal with in Beijing. This particular conjunction of developments provides a moment of opportunity in cross-Strait relations that holds out the possibility of reducing cross-Strait conflict as a potential incendiary device in regional stability. The challenge facing the new U.S. administration is how to overcome the twin perceptions of either trying to build relations with Beijing at Taipei's expense, or vice versa. Strategically, this may provide the single-largest upside possibility in U.S. foreign policy for the new administration, in an admittedly dreary international landscape — which includes wars in Iraq and Afghanistan, shaky relations with Russia, volatile interactions with Iran, and a dismal U.S. global image. In his inaugural address, Taiwan's new president invited a change in thinking saying that, "what matters is not sovereignty but core values and way of life."

The opportunity for the stabilization of cross-Strait relations and therefore broader regional stability, a truly important strategic gain for the United States, arises from the fact that as of May 20, 2008, the people of Taiwan have a Kuomintang (KMT) government in control of the legislative and executive branches. This reduces the divided-government gridlock of the preceding eight years that effectively killed any possibility of significant forward motion. The post-May 20, 2008 government replaces a Democratic Progressive Party (DPP)-led administration that spent eight years conducting identity politics and hesitated to deepen cross-Strait economic and social interaction for fear it would constrain autonomy, and block ultimate independence.

As indicated by President Ma Ying-jeou's inauguration speech, the visit of KMT Chairman Wu Poh-hsiung to the mainland shortly thereafter, and the June agreement on direct charter flights; the new administration in Taipei has delicately subscribed to the so-called "1992 Consensus" that vaguely affirms a one China approach. The KMT and its leaders see Taiwan's economic welfare at stake in growing economic interaction with the mainland — reflected in talk and action with respect to increased direct trade and transportation, currency exchange, augmented tourism, and more investment across the Strait. In short, the new government in Taipei wants to improve cross-Strait relations and stabilize ties for a considerable period — moves profoundly in America's interests. This brings us to the mainland.

In Beijing, Hu Jintao's second-term administration represents an evolution from earlier policies of forceful "liberation" in the 1950s and 1960s, through the policy of "peaceful reunification, one country, two systems" (with the emphasis on reunification), to the current implicit, more modest, and more feasible objective of "no (de jure) independence" for the island. The mainland is as focused on its own staggering internal agenda as Washington is focused on its problems internationally (not to mention, domestically). Beijing wants and needs to stabilize the cross-Strait situation so it can focus inward on true regime threats. This is the underlying reason why President Hu Jintao, in his report to the 17th Party Congress of October 2007, expressed his hope to reach "a final end to the state of hostility between the two sides [of the Taiwan Strait], reach a peace agreement, construct a framework for peaceful development of cross-Straits relations, and thus usher in a new phase of peaceful development."

And in Washington, almost irrespective of which political party or individual wins the White House (and Congress) in the November

2008 elections, the United States will not be looking for tension or conflict in the Taiwan Strait. The United States will have to take account of its ever-growing strategic stakes in cooperating on transnational and proliferation issues with Beijing; while adjusting to the fact that China is America's fastest-growing major export market, a major U.S. creditor, and an engine of the world economy. Of course, there may be an after-wash of possible major weapons sale(s) to Taipei by the George W. Bush administration to deal with, as there may be some legacy of unhelpful campaign-trail rhetoric to overcome, but these developments are unlikely (in isolation) to fundamentally change the opportunities discussed here.

Beijing wants and needs to stabilize the cross-Strait situation so it can focus inward on true regime threats.

The new administration in Washington should delicately, but vigorously, seize the above-mentioned alignment of stars in each capital to encourage and facilitate the long-term stabilization of cross-Strait relations — realizing that Beijing and Taipei have to take the initiative, that progress will take time, and that too assertive a role by Washington would likely be counterproductive. The lodestar for policy should be the one articulated by Secretary of State George P. Shultz in March 1987 — "Our steadfast policy seeks to foster an environment in which such developments can continue to take place."

Among the many questions this circumstance raises are two of particular significance: 1) What are U.S. interests in various cross-Strait outcomes? And 2) what can the United States do, if anything, to nudge things in a constructive direction?

Among the many questions this circumstance raises are two of particular significance: 1) What are U.S. interests in various cross-Strait outcomes? And 2) what can the United States do, if anything, to nudge things in a constructive direction?

U.S. Interests?

The definition of "U.S. interests" is shaped by analysts' varied values and definitions of the situation — consequently, it is not always objectively obvious what is in "America's interests." Moreover, short and long-term interests may diverge. A China that is a responsible international stakeholder and has progressively more humane, law-based, and pluralistic governance is a China in which everyone can have more confidence. In some sense, what is in U.S. interests depends on the character of the future China.

With these caveats accepted, one can begin thinking about "U.S. interests" by considering the Taiwan Relations Acts of April 1979. In this U.S. law, core American interests were defined (by the U.S. Congress, agreed to by then-President Carter, and subsequently reaffirmed by five successive administrations) as follows: "to help maintain peace, security, and stability in the Western Pacific; and…the continuation of commercial, cultural, and other relations between the people of the United States and the people of Taiwan." Clearly, a long-term framework for cross-Strait peace — that stabilized the situation in the Strait and left

Taiwan free to deal with the rest of the world commercially, culturally, and otherwise — would meet this basic test.

U.S. credibility among friends and allies in the region and beyond increasingly requires that Washington show the capacity to manage the cross-Strait situation in a way that progressively reduces the dangers that they (U.S. allies) would be drawn into an unnecessary and counterproductive cross-Strait conflict. Increasingly, U.S. allies (Japan and the Republic of Korea most notably) find that China is their number-one export market; and they seek to balance their interests between Washington and Beijing, rather than blindly following Washington into a conflict in the Taiwan Strait, as Deputy Secretary of State Richard Armitage found out in 2001 when he traveled to Australia. Whereas in the Cold War "standing up to Beijing" is what it took to achieve credibility and unity of purpose with our allies, increasingly, the capacity to manage the relationship with Beijing in a productive fashion is what is required to be credible in the new era. The U.S. image in Asia would be enhanced if Washington could somehow contribute to a long-term stabilization of a situation that has been a major regional worry for nearly six decades. Australia and the Republic of Korea are only the two most obvious examples of allies who ardently wish not to choose between Beijing and Washington in the context of a Taiwan conflict.

Another take on U.S. interests simply requires one to look at the overall context — China is becoming economically and strategically more important to the United States at a considerable rate; no significant transnational problem (e.g., global warming, energy, proliferation, or global infectious diseases) can be handled without its cooperation. As the benefits of cooperation continually grow, the costs of a head-on collision grow as well. Increasingly, therefore, without cross-Strait stability, Washington will find itself making ever-bigger commitments to offset China's growing strength – to defend relatively smaller and smaller interests in Taiwan – at the expense of strategically central cooperation with Beijing.

Whereas in the Cold War "standing up to Beijing" is what it took to achieve credibility and unity of purpose with our allies, increasingly, the capacity to manage the relationship with Beijing in a productive fashion is what is required to be credible in the new era.

And finally, the United States (in some sense like China) desperately needs to focus on its own internal tasks such as deficit reduction, rebuilding and expanding physical and human infrastructure, developing new energy sources, funding social security for a rapidly expanding group of retirees, improving education for K-12 students, and constraining health care costs to a tolerable percentage of gross domestic product (GDP).

Cumulatively, these interests require that the United States at least be supportive of both sides of the Taiwan Strait in their efforts to stabilize cross-Strait relations. The question is how to do so without sparking the anxieties of either or both sides of the Strait?

Recommendations and Conclusions: How (If At All) Can the U.S. Contribute to Long-Term Stabilization of the Strait?

As Secretary Shultz said more than 20 years ago with respect to cross-Strait tension reduction: "The pace, however, will be determined by the Chinese on either side of the Taiwan Strait, free of outside pressure." If I were to amend this in light of developments since 1987, it would be with respect to only the last clause. President Bill Clinton and George W. Bush's administrations forcefully enunciated American interests when Beijing or Taipei threatened to upset the status-quo in ways highly adverse to U.S. interests — the former president by sending aircraft carriers to the waters off Taiwan in 1996, and the latter by trying repeatedly to restrain then-Taiwan President Chen Shui-bian. The United States has interests and should not be shy about articulating them. But, as these two examples suggest, Washington needs to be careful that the mere acts of deterring or reassuring one of the cross-Strait parties do not fuel the counterproductive anxieties, or reckless behavior, of the other. The Clinton administration's efforts to reassure then-Taiwan President Lee Teng-hui by issuing him a visa to go to Cornell University in 1995 aroused destabilizing behavior from Beijing in 1995-96 (firing missiles); which in turn necessitated efforts to deter Beijing by sending carriers. These moves (and the early statements of President Bush) emboldened Chen Shui-bian to ignore Washington's equities, and those of the entire region in a variety of ways. Consequently, the administration of George W. Bush spent most of its two terms trying to limit the dangers presented by an emboldened Democratic Progressive Party (DPP) president.

One of the first actions a new administration should take is to articulate a framework for its overall China policy, which includes Taiwan. Such a framework would contribute to building a base of public and congressional understanding in which the day-to-day frictions and opportunities with China can be placed within the larger perspective of tradeoffs, costs, and gains. With respect to Beijing and Taipei, such a framework creates added confidence that the new administration is not in an opportunistic, reactive mode. The administration of George W. Bush did not articulate a coherent, comprehensive presidential statement on China in its first seven years. The best, most comprehensive and forward-looking statement of that administration was given by then-Deputy Secretary of State Robert Zoellick in September 2005 — five years into the Bush presidency. The Zoellick statement represents a good starting point for the next U.S. administration. A key part of such a framework should be focusing U.S.-China relations on the strategic task of cooperatively addressing the huge spillovers from China's modernization and transnational problems.[1]

One of the first actions a new administration should take is to articulate a framework for its overall China policy, which includes Taiwan.

Second, in the current circumstance, there is no reason to fiddle with any of the underlying major documents that have structured the U.S.-China relationship since the Shanghai Communiqué of February 1972 (including the Normalization Communiqué of December 1979, the August 1982 Communiqué on arms sales, and the April 1979 Taiwan Relations Act). But, it might be useful for the new president to make it clear early in his administration that the United States sees no incompatibility between its own interests and ever closer mainland-Taiwan cooperation.

Third, Washington (including the administration of George W. Bush) should encourage Beijing to make some meaningful moves that will give Taiwan's new President, Ma Ying-jeou, some added capital with his own people. In his inaugural address, Ma took several steps forward by expressing a willingness to proceed with the People's Republic of China on the basis of the "1992 Consensus"; introducing a note of flexibility about the dead-end argument over sovereignty; expressing a willingness to move forward with the mainland on the basis of "no unification, no independence, and no use of force"; and moving away from Chen Shui-bian's efforts to de-sinify the island, by referring to the "common Chinese heritage" of both sides of the Strait. It will be much easier for President Ma to respond to a meaningful Chinese move.

One such move, for instance, would be to a find a way for Taiwan to meaningfully participate in the functional work of the World Health Assembly/Organization (WHO) in an appropriate status, subsequently proceeding to other organizations for which statehood is not a requirement. Such a gesture by Beijing, when added to movement already underway on cross-Strait transportation, tourism, investment, taxation, and foreign exchange, could give cross-Strait relations considerable momentum.

And finally, a new administration ought to remind Beijing and Taipei that U.S. security and weapons activities in the Taiwan Strait have always been tied to the cross-Strait threat and that a lower threat level would result in less need for U.S. security-related concern and actions, including weapons sales. In this vein, the George W. Bush administration never did explore Chinese President Jiang Zemin's intimation in Crawford, Texas, in October

2002 that U.S. restraint in arms sales might result in reduced numbers of missiles aimed in Taiwan's direction. In the context of a cross-Strait peace framework by Beijing and Taipei, such U.S.-China discussions would presumably be appropriate. In the meantime, to signal its cooperative intentions, Beijing should announce an indefinite "freeze" in new missile deployments, perhaps simultaneously asking for comparable restraint in Taiwan and elsewhere.

---

[1] David M. Lampton, *The Three Faces of Chinese Power: Might, Money, and Minds* (Berkeley, CA: University of California Press, 2008).

U.S.-JAPAN RELATIONS: WHAT SHOULD WASHINGTON DO?

Ralph A. Cossa

Issue: The new post-Cold War generation of leaders that is emerging in Japan must find ways to reinvigorate the Japanese economy, gain the international stature Japanese feel they deserve, and cope with the challenge of China's growing influence and power in the region. Many U.S. leaders take Japan for granted and are only dimly aware, if at all, of the frustrations Japanese feel as they seek to determine what strategy can best address these challenges. Moreover, coordination in successive U.S. administrations of the political, economic, and security aspects of the U.S.-Japan relationship has been less than optimal. Are there actions a new U.S. administration can take that would put this vital relationship on a sound footing for the next decade or more?

Introduction

To a casual outside observer, the relationship between Japan and the United States today seems quite sound. If one compares where the relationship stood at the beginning of this decade and then measures how far it has come, one could argue that the situation evolved from the "Japan bashing" and "Japan passing" of the 1990s to "Japan surpassing" under former Prime Minister Koizumi Junichiro. But this is only half the picture.

The Bush-Koizumi heyday was a tremendous ride, but it is over. It saw "boots on the ground" (Japanese troop deployments to Iraq) and "boats in the bay" as Japan initiated and, with some political difficulty and a brief hiatus, renewed its maritime refueling support to allied forces prosecuting the global war on terrorism in Afghanistan. In retrospect, the relationship peaked in February 2005 with the signing of the 2+2 Joint Statement, which laid out, for the first time, common security objectives for the alliance. Few expected the post-9/11 momentum of the U.S.-Japan relationship to be sustained post-Koizumi, but the manner in which it has sputtered to a halt has arguably brought about another era of "Japan bashing." This time, however, the Japanese are doing the self-flagellation.

In March 2008, at the 14th annual Pacific Forum Center for Strategic and International Studies (CSIS) Japan-U.S. Security Seminar in San Francisco, the Japanese participants had growing questions about Tokyo's future contribution to the alliance and to regional and global stability — given political inertia at home and the perceived relative decline in Japanese prestige and influence abroad, especially vis-a-vis an ever-rising China. The sharpest concern was that Tokyo would begin to backslide and be unable or unwilling to implement agreements already reached, or to pursue objectives already outlined.

The remedy must come primarily from Tokyo, but there is much Washington can do – or refrain from doing – that can help revitalize the alliance and restore Japanese confidence in themselves and in their primary ally.

First and foremost, Washington must better understand that it has contributed to the current state of insecurity and uneasiness in Tokyo. At a Pacific Forum U.S.-Japan Strategic Dialogue in

February 2008, there was strong consensus among senior Japanese security experts (including a number of government officials acting in their private capacities) that Washington appears to be a less reliable ally today than it was during the Koizumi era.

Some of the rationale for this perception should not come as a surprise: Japanese politicians and the public alike have voiced strong displeasure over their perception of a "sudden reversal" in U.S. policy toward North Korea in February 2007. This specifically pertains to a feeling of betrayal over the abductee issue; the perceived lack of enthusiasm from Washington regarding Tokyo's bid for a permanent UN Security Council seat; and the Honda Amendment, which called on Japan to apologize to World War II comfort women. The latter, especially, was seen as an insult to a loyal ally that had bucked severe political pressure at home to contribute unprecedented resources in Iraq and Afghanistan.

The assured ultimate rejection of Japan's request for F-22 aircraft is another case in point. While Americans see this as part of a global position – we do not sell F-22s to any ally – the Japanese have taken it personally, especially after reading a Congressional Research Service report, which cautioned against the sale due to the negative impact it would have on Sino-U.S. relations. While a negative Chinese reaction may not be a significant factor from Washington's point of view – it would likely gain votes for the sale both in the Pentagon and the halls of Congress – to nervous Japanese, this is more evidence of a feared U.S. tilt toward China, which lies at the heart of Japanese insecurity today.

There is an Asian — and especially Japanese — perception that China has already eclipsed Japan economically, despite Beijing's very ambitious economic forecasts that peg 2020 as the year when China will reach the current size of Japan's economy. This has led more and more countries in Asia to bandwagon with — and cautiously hedge against — a rising China. Subsequently, Tokyo is feeling increasingly isolated in Asia, which makes the perception of the U.S. as an unreliable ally all the more fearsome. One suspects that much of the talk in Japan about "values-based diplomacy" is aimed not at "containing" China but at reminding Washington of the difference between Japan and China and who would be the more suitable and reliable partner. There is a zero sum nature to this that is lost on most Americans who rightly believe that Washington can and should have good relations with both countries, and that one does not preclude the other.

Subsequently, Tokyo is feeling increasingly isolated in Asia, which makes the perception of the U.S. as an unreliable ally all the more fearsome.

For Tokyo, Washington's strategic overtures toward New Delhi are also troubling for a variety of reasons, including its long-standing commitment to nuclear disarmament and the Nuclear Non-Proliferation Treaty (NPT), which India continues to reject. More importantly, Japanese wonder if Washington's rationale for accepting India as a de facto nuclear weapons state – that India is a democracy which can be trusted – points to an eventual similar acquiescence should democratic South Korea develop nuclear weapons or inherit those currently being tolerated in the North. When Tokyo tried to suggest the need for a values-based multilateral concert involving Washington, Canberra, New Delhi, and Tokyo, the lack of enthusiasm from the other three capitals added insult to injury.

The Japanese decrease of faith in themselves and in their U.S. ally could have serious strategic implications. For the past two years, thoughtful voices have been raised in government and academic circles about the extent and reliability of America's extended deterrence. Can Washington really be relied upon in the event of nuclear, chemical, or biological attack from North Korea? Worse yet, is Washington sending signals that it is apathetic about Japan becoming a nuclear power? The Japanese are debating whether or not to have the debate; influential Japanese are emphasizing that Tokyo's decision not to pursue a nuclear option is the product of a simple cost-benefit analysis. Today, the costs of pursuing this option far outweigh the perceived benefits. But, a major determinant is the amount of faith Tokyo has in Washington's reliability.

This essay does not predict an alliance breakdown between the United States and Japan. Even if the above concerns are left unattended, the alliance will likely continue to muddle through; and it would take a great shock to push Japan over the nuclear edge. For more than 40 years, the Japanese have needed reassurance of a U.S. commitment to the bilateral relationship—but recent references by many U.S. officials and the presidential candidates to the U.S.-China relationship as the "most important" bilateral relationship have amplified Japanese insecurity. We ignore this at our own peril.

Recommendations and Conclusions

There are a number of steps the next U.S. administration could take to reduce the current level of Japanese anxiety and help reinvigorate the U.S.-Japan alliance.

First, 2010 marks the 50th anniversary of the San Francisco Treaty, which seems like an appropriate opportunity to create a new vision statement that outlines our common strategic objectives for the next half century. Highlighting 2010 now as a point for alliance renewal will help drive the revitalization process. This, however, should not delay the next administration in taking immediate concrete steps to reinvigorate the alliance in 2009, which includes making a joint commitment to accomplish all the unfinished tasks presently agreed upon but not yet implemented.

2010 marks the 50th anniversary of the San Francisco Treaty,

which seems like an appropriate opportunity to create

a new vision statement that outlines our common strategic

objectives for the next half century.

For Washington, these unfinished tasks are important. However, all too often, Americans focus on tactical issues such as the Defense Policy Review Initiative (DPRI) and earlier Special Action Committee on Okinawa (SACO) commitments; in addition to existing challenges like the relocation of forces to Guam, host nation support, and status of forces agreement (SOFA) modifications, etc. The new U.S. administration must begin to focus on a broader strategic context; a vision statement and a resumption of the U.S.-Japan Strategic Dialogue would help accomplish this task.

Second, U.S.-Japan policy in 2009 and a 2010 vision statement of the alliance's future should focus on broadening and deepening the bilateral relationship to make it more suitable and viable in the

21st Century. As the world's two richest and most technologically advanced countries, we should be more closely coordinating our democracy promotion, economic reform efforts, and our overseas economic and security assistance, while expanding our focus to include non-traditional security challenges. A Japan-U.S. Free Trade Agreement would be mutually beneficial and help bind our economies together. This, however, should not be negotiated unless and until Washington is once again prepared to see such initiatives come to fruition, so as to avoid embarrassing missteps like those taken with the U.S.-Korea Free Trade Agreement (FTA). Washington and Tokyo must also be on the same side when promoting the Doha Agenda and future Asia-Pacific Economic Cooperation (APEC) initiatives, such as the Asia-Pacific FTA.

Third, any U.S.-Japan bilateral dialogue needs a common definition both within and between Tokyo and Washington when referring to a "normal" Japan. Today, common understanding about what Japan really seeks to become or what Washington desires it to be is lacking. Japan's neighbors have a very different definition of the term, and their concerns and suspicions also need to be addressed. The nature of the U.S.-Japan alliance has changed dramatically in the past decade, but the explanation of it has not. In the 1980s and early 1990s, one U.S. official characterized it as "keeping Japan in a box that it wanted to stay in." Today, one could describe it as "helping Japan out of a box that it wants to get out of." With Japanese troops in Iraq and a resumption of non-combat support to Afghanistan combat operations, Tokyo clearly has at least one foot out of the box. What is missing is a clear articulation by Tokyo and by Washington of Japan's future role and aspirations once it is fully out of the box. We must have a common vision of what constitutes a "normal" Japan and the role it rightly aspires to play in East Asia and beyond. Developing and explaining this vision to domestic audiences in the United States and Japan — and gaining acceptance of it from Japan's neighbors — are key future alliance challenges that must be overcome.

Fourth, any future vision statement will require a mutual strategy toward China. Most Japanese, as well as Chinese and others in the Asian region, would be relieved if the Bush administration's "responsible stakeholder" concept[1] were to carry over into the next administration. Coordination with the Japanese government and subsequent Japanese public buy-in on the new U.S. administration's first major China address would significantly help in correcting the perception that the U.S. "tilts" toward China.

In the category of regional security architecture and cooperation, the U.S.-Japan relationship is central, as it provides the foundation upon which to build a constructive relationship with a rising China and Asia region. However, in the category of regional (if not global) security, Sino-U.S. relations are equally important, as missteps in this relationship could contribute to a new bipolar world. Japanese certainly realize and accept this proposition, but when the U.S.-China relationship is rhetorically established as the "most important" for the U.S., it feeds Japanese anxiety. U.S. leaders must be cognizant of this.

Fifth, the time is ripe for three-way, official dialogue among Washington, Tokyo, and Beijing. Washington and Tokyo used to favor such dialogue, with Beijing dragging its heels. Now, the Chinese are openly suggesting such a forum, with Washington hesitating. Having a formal three-way dialogue helps elevate Japan's position as an equal partner in East Asia security affairs; this should be welcome in both Washington and Tokyo. Seoul will have suspicions about such a trilateral dialogue and care should be given in addressing them. A reinvigoration of the old Trilateral Coordination and Oversight Group (TCOG) — which previously helped keep Washington, Tokyo, and Seoul on the same page in dealing with North Korea — should help satisfy Seoul.

Sixth, the opportunity also seems ripe for improved bilateral relations between Tokyo and Seoul, with a new, more receptive leadership in Seoul and a less nationalistic one in Tokyo. Washington should be an active facilitator in this regard. President Bush missed a great opportunity, during his Camp David Summit with ROK President Lee Myung-Bak, when he failed to publicly spell out the importance of a close Korea-Japan bilateral relationship and even closer trilateral coordination with the U.S., in dealing with both North Korea and in promoting regional stability in general. This would have been a natural point to make, given that Lee's next stop was Tokyo. Likewise, when the next U.S. president visits Japan, he should make a point of reminding Japanese of how important good relations with Korea are to their own stability. More importantly, a similar message should be delivered whenever a U.S. president visits Seoul. Historically, this has not been done.

Seventh, the next president's first trip abroad (perhaps even as president-elect) should be to Asia, with Tokyo as the first stop.

Eighth, greater transparency is needed regarding U.S. policy toward North Korea, the Japanese government's greatest concern. Here, Washington used to argue that it would not negotiate bilaterally with Pyongyang because it enabled the North to play one side against the other and to weaken the bond among the other five members of the six-party process at a time when speaking with one voice was crucial. Current bilateral dialogue between the United States and North Korea is validating this concern. Japanese are becoming increasingly suspicious of secret deals made in Berlin, Singapore, and elsewhere, and see what they perceive as firm commitments from the president and other senior U.S. officials being adjusted or abandoned.

All six parties were, together, supposed to be negotiating the removal of nuclear weapons from North Korea. But it is widely perceived that the United States and the DPRK are now negotiating the nuclear issue during their bilateral working group sessions, while the other four are merely advised of the process when they meet in plenary sessions. U.S.-DPRK talks may be more efficient, but their impact on bilateral trust has been severe. Washington must acknowledge this and find a better way to keep its Japanese ally reliably engaged. We must clearly articulate how we define "sufficient progress" on the abductee issue and be more precise about promises and linkages — at least privately but, to the maximum extent possible, publicly as well.

Ninth, given growing Japanese concerns about the reliability of Washington's extended deterrence and its nuclear policies in general, the United States must discover a way to engage Tokyo in a nuclear dialogue in advance of the next U.S. Nuclear Posture Review, which the next administration is mandated by Congress to produce. This would assure Tokyo that Japanese concerns are being taken into account as Washington makes future decisions regarding its deterrence posture, missile defense, and other issues that are critical to Japan's national security. While direct dialogue between the Japanese Ministry of Defense and the U.S. Department of Defense would be best, a closed track-two or track-1.5 dialogue might also serve this purpose.

Tenth, Washington and Tokyo must finally define what the global nature of their partnership entails. Japan has critical interests in the Middle East and has more entry than Washington into Iran and other countries where U.S. relationships are cold. Yet Japanese requests for a seat at the table in the Permanent 5 Plus One (Germany) Talks have fallen on deaf ears. Of course, Tokyo has not done a very good job in explaining its value if invited, but if Japan is supposed to be "the United Kingdom of Asia,"[2] then it needs to be consulted on global issues that impact it. After years of telling Japan to "step up to the plate," Washington now seems reluctant to let Tokyo play in the big league — and Tokyo seems confused as to what position it would like to play. A true strategic dialogue is needed — one in which Washington listens as well as speaks, and Tokyo asserts its strategic and tactical value.

Finally, the next U.S. administration must develop and articulate an East Asia strategy that puts Washington's relations with Japan, China, and other Asian countries into broader perspective. The East Asia Security Initiative (EASI) and East Asia Strategy Review (EASR), documents produced by the George H. W. Bush and Clinton administrations respectively, provide much needed context to American force restructuring in the post-Cold War environment, but there has been no update since 1998. Asia, in the meantime, has changed dramatically. After completing the National Security Strategy and the National Military Strategy Reports, the new U.S. administration should produce a new East Asia strategy report to provide context and reassurance of the U.S. commitment to the Asian region as a whole.[3]

---

[1] The "responsible stakeholder" phrase was coined by then-Deputy Secretary of State Robert Zoellick, to encourage China to work within the system and to remind Beijing that it would be judged by its actions (support to rogue states, etc.). See, for example, Zoellick's comments during the Second U.S.-China Senior Dialogue in Washington DC in

December 2005, when he remarked, 'As it becomes a major global player, we are now encouraging China to become a "responsible stakeholder" that will work with the United States and others to sustain, adapt, and advance the peaceful international system that has enabled its success.'

2   It is worth noting that the "UK of Asia" analogy has been overused and misunderstood. As originally described by former Deputy Secretary of State Richard Armitage, it was intended to simply note that the U.S. would never think about conducting a major global initiative, much less one in Europe, without first consulting the British; and that Tokyo should likewise be consulted first, especially regarding actions or policy changes dealing with Asia. The phrase did not intend to promote Japanese combat operations or nuclear weapons. A more accurate analogy is Japan as "Germany, ten years removed." In the first Gulf War, the world was not ready for German troops. Berlin sent ships to the Mediterranean to free up other NATO forces for combat operations against Iraq. Japan wrote a (large) check! Ten years later, German combat troops are on the ground in Afghanistan while Japanese ships were (and are) providing logistical support in the Indian Ocean, thus freeing up U.S. and other ships for combat operations against Iraq. Perhaps in another 10 years, Japanese combat operations will be acceptable to both the Japanese people and the international community (although one hopes no conflict will arise to test this hypothesis).

3   The Pacific Forum, working with four Washington D.C.-based institutes – Center for Naval Analysis (CAN), Institute for Defense Analysis (IDA), Institute of National Security Strategy (INSS), and Center for a New American Security (CNAS) – is working on a draft of such a document for consideration by the next administration.

U.S. RELATIONS WITH THE KOREAN PENINSULA: RECOMMENDATIONS FOR A NEW ADMINISTRATION

Scott Snyder

Issue: In the absence of a dramatic breakthrough in the Six-Party Talks on the North Korean nuclear issue, a new U.S. administration will urgently need to address the question of what policies to adopt to maximize prospects for success on the denuclearization issue, and how to deal with the consequences of failure. Determining the right approach must be addressed against the backdrop of Korean hopes for eventual reunification – hopes that rose sharply during the heyday of the "sunshine" policy. Koreans are also wrestling with the question of how to position themselves to maximize their regional influence and to enhance their political, economic, and security interests. Are present U.S. policies adequate for the purpose of securing U.S. interests in Northeast Asia or do these policies need to be recalibrated; and if so, in what fashion? To what extent will engagement with North Korea further U.S. and South Korean goals? Should a U.S. goal be to seek a six-party stabilization arrangement in Northeast Asia?

Introduction

Despite the Bush administration's continuing efforts to negotiate North Korea's denuclearization, it is increasingly clear that the challenges posed by a nuclear-capable North Korea under Kim Jong-Il will be passed on to a new administration in January 2009. If disablement of North Korea's Yongbyon facility proceeds and North Korea provides only a partial declaration of facilities constituting its nuclear program, the next American president will inherit the task of completing North Korea's full denuclearization.

Even if disablement of the Yongbyon facility is successfully concluded by the year's end, the unfinished business of full denuclearization will remain as a paradoxical challenge for a new team of policymakers: the urgency of an immediate crisis surrounding North Korea's nuclear program will have dissipated, but the core objective of the Bush administration to reverse North Korea's nuclear program rather than simply freezing it as the Clinton administration had done will not be achieved. The failure is compounded by the fact that the Bush administration allowed North Korea to acquire enough plutonium for a small nuclear arsenal following Pyongyang's October 2006 nuclear test.

Despite its relatively stable appearance, the Bush administration is likely to hand off to its successors a situation that remains dangerous. The immediate crisis associated with North Korea's continued acquisition of nuclear weapons-grade materials will have been contained; but the inherited status quo would imply acceptance of North Korea as a de facto nuclear power, thereby allowing it to evade commitments made at Six-Party Talks to implement denuclearization. The groundwork laid by Christopher Hill at the Six-Party Talks offers a reasonable foundation for continued pursuit of a diplomatic approach under the February 13, 2007 implementing agreement and the September 19, 2005 Six Party Joint Statement. Although these efforts have begun to bring North Korea's program back under control, a new U.S. administration might find itself in a stronger position than the current one to utilize effective coordination with other participants in the Six-Party Talks and U.S.-DPRK negotiations. But a new president may also face a more contentious political environment at home and less political support for implementation of commitments necessary to achieve North Korea's full denuclearization.

Despite its relatively stable appearance, the Bush administration is likely to hand off to its successors a situation that remains dangerous.

By changing the tone of the U.S. approach to North Korea and taking advantage of the opportunity to reinvigorate U.S.-ROK alliance coordination, a new administration will be in a stronger position and have the potential to accomplish far more than the Bush administration. This can be achieved by building on efforts already underway to resolve five apparent contradictions that have limited the Bush administration's efforts to address North Korea's nuclear challenge:

1. The challenge of dealing with North Korea juxtaposed with America's broader policy toward Asia.

2. The relationship between America's Asian alliances and the Six-Party Talks, and the development of a regional security dialogue.

3. The relationship between U.S.-DPRK bilateral talks and six-party negotiations.

4. The pursuit of negotiations with North Korea in equal measure with contingency planning for possible political instability in the DPRK.

5. The relationship between North Korea's denuclearization, and U.S.-DPRK diplomatic normalization and peace on the Korean peninsula.

By changing the tone of the U.S. approach to North Korea and taking advantage of the opportunity to reinvigorate U.S.-ROK alliance coordination, a new administration will be in a stronger position and have the potential to accomplish far more than the Bush administration.

A Changed Tone in Rhetoric

A new U.S. president will have the opportunity to leave behind the negative tone set by President Bush's initial, negative remarks toward North Korea and its leadership by affirming that if both sides are able to overcome mistrust and improve the relationship by developing a shared record of performance through the principle of "action for action," relations can improve. A softening of rhetoric will strengthen U.S. credibility and leverage vis-à-vis North Korea and other participants in the six-party negotiations, but should not prevent a willingness to utilize coercive tools if necessary.

A softening of rhetoric will strengthen U.S. credibility and lever-

age vis-à-vis North Korea and other participants in the six-party

negotiations, but should not prevent a willingness to utilize coer-

cive tools if necessary.

At the same time, it should be made clear that the United States will not sacrifice its principles, ideals, or norms in the areas of democracy or human rights that have been accepted and under-scored in accordance with the minimum standards of the international community. The United States should not allow North Korea to be exempted from such international standards of conduct, nor should it attempt to provide Pyongyang with special favors that might have the effect of propping up the regime. At the same time, it should not stand in the way of North Korea receiving the benefits of enhanced integration with the rest of the world if it meets these responsibilities. A new administration will have an opportunity to utilize the foundations laid by the Bush administration to carry out an integrative, multi-track policy toward North Korea that overcomes many of the critical contradictions that have hobbled Bush administration efforts.

Reinvigorate U.S.-ROK Alliance Coordination

The new South Korean president Lee Myung-bak has emphasized his willingness to pursue a unified U.S.-ROK approach toward North Korea and has stated that strengthening the U.S.-ROK alliance will also be helpful to North Korea. Lee's emphasis on the U.S.-ROK alliance as a priority and as a foundation for strengthened coordination of policy toward North Korea helps close the gap between diplomatic approaches that existed under his predecessor, Roh Moo-hyun. Effective coordination of policy approaches toward North Korea will create a tremendous opportunity to expand U.S.-ROK alliance cooperation to include global, regional, and non-traditional security issues. South Korea's expanded capacity as the world's twelfth largest economy, and the convergence of social and political attitudes between the United States as a result of South Korea's political development and economic growth have raised the potential for U.S.-ROK bilateral cooperation to a much broader level than was previously thought possible. In the course of redefining and expanding a shared vision for promoting global stability and the unconventional global threats emerging, the United States and South Korea should work closely together to achieve North Korea's denuclearization and promote lasting stability on the Korean peninsula.

Recommendations and Conclusions

1. Make North Korea a centerpiece for reaffirming the effectiveness of American leadership in Northeast Asia.

North Korea's nuclear weapons program represents the single biggest challenge to the collective security interests of major players in Northeast Asia. But the inability of any party to resolve the issue independent of U.S. involvement became clear despite President Bush's categorization of the North Korean nuclear challenge as a "regional problem." Concerned parties universally called upon the United States to actively address this issue, underscoring the need for U.S. leadership to effectively address one of Asia's most critical regional security challenges. The lack of a clearly articulated U.S. policy toward Asia as a region has further underscored doubts and frustrations.

The lack of a clearly articulated U.S. policy toward Asia as a region has further underscored doubts and frustrations.

The United States can reaffirm and expand its role as a regional stabilizer in Asia by committing military resources and political leadership to address North Korea's nuclear program. Effective mobilization of region-wide diplomatic efforts to address the political and security problems deriving from North Korea's nuclear pursuits can contribute to effective management of North Korea as a source of instability that concerns all of its neighbors; while also underscoring the vitality and relevance of U.S. leadership in effectively addressing Asia's core political and security problems.

The effective exercise of U.S. leadership will underscore U.S. cooperation with China, Russia, and other regional players while simultaneously reaffirming America's leading role at a time when many have suggested that Asia's rising economic interdependence might marginalize U.S. regional influence. To the extent that the United States alone is able to mobilize the collective political will to effectively manage North Korea's nuclear weapons pursuits, regional partners will continue to look to it as an indispensable leader in Asian regional affairs. Effective U.S. leadership would also ensure that the United States is able to maximize its influence beyond the North Korean nuclear issue — for instance, by ensuring that the establishment of any multilateral dialogue mechanism, such as the

Northeast Asia Peace and Security Mechanism (NEAPSM) that has been proposed as part of the Six-Party Talks, would be influenced by and consistent with a strong U.S. role.

2. Forge a common position with allies regarding the DPRK's denuclearization and development in support of regional/ multilateral efforts via Six-Party Talks.

A new administration can restore trilateral policy coordination with Japan and South Korea as a basis for dealing more effectively with the DPRK and as the core of six-party efforts to address the North Korean nuclear issue. Although some have argued that trilateral coordination is no longer necessary in light of the Six-Party Talks or somehow challenges the six-party framework, a new administration must work to correct this misperception. Past U.S. policy toward North Korea has been most successful when the United States, Japan, and South Korea have been on the same page. The high point of such cooperation occurred in the context of the Perry process in 1998-99 with the establishment of the Trilateral Coordination and Oversight Group (TCOG).

Such coordination would not hold bilateral developments in any of the respective relationships with Pyongyang hostage to trilateral consultations, or vice versa. Coordination strengthens the possibility that progress in one relationship can promote a "virtuous circle" of progress in other bilateral relationships with the DPRK. The most effective tools for inducing progress with North Korea thus far have been related to the withholding of promised benefits to the North contingent upon its performance, rather than threats of negative retaliation against North Korea. Close political coordination among the United States, Japan, and South Korea is necessary to show political will through coordination of such an approach and to prevent North Korea from exploiting differences among allies.

3. Harmonize the relationship between U.S.-DPRK bilateral negotiations and coordination among the six parties.

During the past year, U.S.-DPRK talks have become the center-piece of the Bush administration's approach to North Korea's denu-clearization to the extent that both Chinese and Japanese analysts have independently expressed anxieties that U.S.-DPRK rap-prochement would be achieved at the expense of their own inter-ests vis-à-vis North Korea. To the extent that the U.S.-DPRK talks serve to further the six-party process, they should be conducted with transparency in a manner that quenches conspiracy theories or the fanning of strategic dilemmas regarding the Korean peninsu-la. Both Japan and China remain concerned about the security implications of a unified Korean peninsula hostile to their interests. Responsible and transparent American diplomacy should mitigate these concerns while also denying North Korea the illusion that it can pursue a strategic relationship with the United States as a foil against the influence of other parties on the Korean peninsula.

To the extent that the U.S.-DPRK talks serve to further the six-party process, they should be conducted with transparency in a manner that quenches conspiracy theories or the fanning of strategic dilemmas regarding the Korean peninsula.

---

4. Pursue negotiation with North Korea in equal measure with contingency planning in response to political instability in the DPRK.

Although North Korea has taken the role of negotiating partner along with all of its neighbors during the Six-Party Talks, negotiations alone will not provide North Korea with a "magic bullet" to guarantee its survival. In fact, North Korea's deteriorating political and economic conditions require each of its neighbors to engage in their own contingency planning for possible political instability in the DPRK. It is also necessary for neighboring states to engage in quiet coordination to plan for such contingencies.

The existence of multi-party negotiations with North Korea should not forestall necessary planning to deal with the possibility of sudden instability, a renewed humanitarian crisis, or regime failure in North Korea. South Korea, China, the United States, Japan, and Russia are regional stakeholders likely to be affected by sudden changes in North Korea, and should be prepared to cooperate as necessary in contingency response and avoid misunderstandings. For instance, the possible emergence of a second food crisis in North Korea as a result of North Korea's chronic governance failures is a matter of direct concern to all of North Korea's neighbors. More coordination in response to humanitarian issues should be promoted regardless of potential objections on political grounds from the North.

5. Strengthen the relationship between North Korea's denuclearization and U.S.-DPRK diplomatic normalization and peace on the Korean peninsula.

The new administration should affirm its willingness to build on the September 19, 2005 Joint Statement and February 13, 2006 implementing agreement by affirming its willingness to pursue diplomatic normalization and end the state of confrontation on the Korean peninsula in return for tangible steps by the North to denuclearize. In practical terms, it is not clear whether the new administration would feel a strong need to insist on immediate explanations from the North regarding its uranium enrichment program, but the new administration should retain a high degree of interest in curbing prospects for North Korean proliferation.

Even if North Korea were to issue a forward-leaning statement on proliferation, the next administration should reinforce efforts to promote effective export control regimes and their implementation around the world. In particular, the next administration should consider how to link U.S.-led Proliferation Security Initiative (PSI) efforts with the need for more effective international enforcement of state obligations under United Nations Security Council Resolution 1540.

Likewise, negotiations to replace the Military Armistice Commission with a permanent peace settlement will require close coordination with South Korean allies, most probably in the context of renewed four-party talks among the United States, China, and the two Koreas. As a practical matter, the two Koreas should take the lead in addressing conventional arms control and border management issues necessary to change the Demilitarized Zone (DMZ) into a true zone of peace. In this context, the United States can provide political guarantees and reassurance to the DPRK regarding its peaceful intentions as well as easing restrictions on multilateral financial institutions on provision of technical assistance and by promoting exchanges so that North Korea can operate more effectively in the international community.

In addition, the next administration should have an interest in renewing missile talks, perhaps in close consultation with Japanese colleagues who are most threatened by the North's capabilities. Such a dialogue existed during the Clinton administration, but efforts to address North Korean missile capabilities have been inactive for almost a decade.

Finally, a change in how the United States uses public rhetoric to define North Korea and its nuclear program might strengthen a new administration's advantage in negotiating the removal of North Korea's existing plutonium weapons and stockpiles in return for promoting North Korea's international development. To the extent that diplomatic normalization proceeds, Kim Jong-Il will seek tangible benefits designed to perpetuate his regime and his rule.

Although it is generally inadvisable to trust the North Koreans with cash, a single exception to this rule of thumb might be a deal to purchase North Korea's plutonium stockpiles, as a way toward a more normal political relationship — based on the model of "preventive defense" missions under former Defense Secretary William Perry to buy out and remove nuclear materials from states in the former Soviet Union in the mid-1990s. Although such an effort would face a political and legal firestorm, the next American president might well consider the politically significant gesture of sending the U.S. Secretary of Defense to North Korea to consummate such a deal.

GROUP THINK: THE CHALLENGE OF U.S.-ASEAN RELATIONS

Catharin Dalpino

Issue: The Association of Southeast Asian Nations has favorably altered the balance of power in East Asia by lending collective weight to the smaller and less powerful countries of Southeast Asia, all of whom now belong to the organization. However, the inclusion of Burma (also known as Myanmar) in the group has complicated the U.S. relationship with ASEAN because of strong congressional opposition to any contacts with that regime. Although U.S. relations with individual members of ASEAN are good, many members of ASEAN believe the United States has been less attentive than other regional countries to the organization. The United States is the only regional country that has not adhered to the ASEAN Treaty of Amity and Cooperation, a prerequisite for participation in the annual East Asia summit meetings. How important a role should ASEAN play in the U.S. approach to the region, and are there steps a new U.S. administration could take that would strengthen U.S. ties to the countries of Southeast Asia?

Half a decade after the pivotal events of September 11, 2001, the United States finds itself in a paradoxical position with Southeast Asia and, more specifically, the Association of Southeast Asian Nations (ASEAN). On the one hand, relations with several Southeast Asian governments have expanded significantly with the U.S.-led global war against terrorism and because of a new awareness in Washington of China's rise in Asia. These two factors sparked a modest renaissance in U.S. bilateral relations with

Southeast Asia. Washington found new common cause with Jakarta, Kuala Lumpur, Singapore, and Manila in initiatives to strengthen intelligence sharing, joint surveillance and police training. Indeed, anti-terrorism was the wedge that enabled the United States to resume military-to-military relations with Indonesia. It has helped to reconfigure and renew the U.S.-Philippines treaty alliance, although it has proved to be more problematic in the U.S.-Thailand alliance because of the violence in southern Thailand in recent years. Counter-terrorism has also created a new and positive, if minor, dimension in relations with Hanoi, Phnom Penh, and Vientiane — one that does not involve the complex legacy of the Vietnam War. U.S. policymakers are not inaccurate when they say that U.S. relations with Southeast Asia have never been better.

But critics make two arguments that diminish, if not entirely contradict, this claim. One is that the global war against terrorism has created a backlash, particularly in Muslim areas of Southeast Asia. Surveys and anecdotal evidence suggest that the image of the United States in the region's domestic populations – the now-cliché loss of "soft power" – has fallen precipitously since the promulgation of the Bush doctrine and the beginning of the Iraq war.

A second, related, argument holds that China has increased its political, economic, and security presence in Southeast Asia because of the current tendency for U.S. policymakers to focus primarily on counter-terrorism in the region. Although Beijing's new Southeast Asia policy essentially coalesced in the 1990s —a nd received a quantum boost with the 1997 Asian economic crisis when China reached out to the most afflicted countries with offers of bilateral assistance — U.S. counter-terrorism policy has no doubt helped Beijing to deepen its engagement in smaller, poorer

Southeast Asian countries where Islamic radicalism is not a major problem: Burma, Cambodia, and Laos.[1]

The growing number of external powers seeking closer ties to Southeast Asia – Japan, Australia, India, Russia, the European Union, as well as China – has caused analysts on both sides of the Pacific to worry that the U.S. presence in the region is diluted by default. A more specific concern is that a regional architecture is emerging which could weaken U.S. power in the region, if not now then at some point in the foreseeable future. Some new regional groups, such as ASEAN Plus Three (APT) seek to draw a sharper line between Asia and the broader Pacific. Others, such as the East Asia Summit (EAS) are more inclusive but require that members adhere to specific regional standards. For all practical purposes, these standards are encapsulated in "the ASEAN way."[2] Recently, adhering to them also required signing the ASEAN Treaty of Amity and Cooperation (TAC).

The ASEAN Solution?

In this changing policy environment, a common prescription for U.S. policy in Southeast Asia is for Washington to engage more deeply with ASEAN as an institution, rather than with individual countries in the region. The justifications for this range from the practical (since many regional structures in Asia are built on an ASEAN foundation) to the symbolic (since closer ties with ASEAN would indicate a stronger commitment to Southeast Asia as a whole).

Notwithstanding the fact that all of Southeast Asia's external partners appear to be strengthening their bilateral as well as multilateral relations in the region, there is some evidence that the United

States is lagging behind in the regional race. Washington is the only regional power not to have signed the TAC, the primary consequence being the exclusion of the United States from the EAS.[3] In addition, although the United States has some regional arrangements with ASEAN as a group – such as the U.S.-ASEAN Trade and Investment Framework Arrangement; the U.S.-ASEAN Enterprise Initiative; and the Joint U.S.-ASEAN Enhanced Partnership – none are as comprehensive or ambitious as ASEAN arrangements in train with China, Japan, and India.

China is particularly prolific in this regard. The landmark Framework Agreement on Comprehensive Economic Cooperation between ASEAN and the People's Republic of China (2003) promises, in theory at least, to create the world's largest free trade area. On the security side, China has forged a joint declaration on conduct with the South China Sea (2002), to quell ASEAN nervousness about growing Chinese naval ambitions; and a sweeping "strategic partnership" with ASEAN (2004) that includes nearly every form of cooperation imaginable, from agriculture to energy to media relations. Japan and India have followed suit in part with comprehensive agreements for economic cooperation with ASEAN, both signed in 2003.

The Balance Sheet

Although the United States officially supports robust engagement with ASEAN, U.S. policymakers often do not hesitate to make clear their views that the two fundamental tenets of the "ASEAN way" – non-interference in the internal affairs of member states and decision-making by consensus – render the group a "talk shop." The new ASEAN Charter—specifically the scuttling of an early draft which would have significantly altered the "ASEAN way"—has done little to change minds in Washington on that score. Nevertheless, new and renewed arguments for a deeper and more sustained U.S. relationship with ASEAN deserve consideration. Many analysts on both sides of the Pacific believe that the election of a new U.S. president – whoever it is – will produce a "bounce" in the American image in Southeast Asia. Both presidential candidates have had direct experience with the region, and have positive profiles there. A more vigorous approach to ASEAN may help to institutionalize and extend that honeymoon period.

Moreover, there is increasing evidence that many Southeast Asians – particularly those in Muslim-majority countries – judge the United States as much for its policies outside the region (Iraq, the Israeli-Palestinian conflict and, potentially, Iran) as for its actions in Southeast Asia.

Without doubt, the United States needs a public relations boost in Southeast Asia, although it is not clear that ASEAN is necessarily the best path to an improved image. If the greatest loss of "soft power" has been with Southeast Asian domestic populations rather than governments, increased participation in an inter-governmental organization may not have an appreciable impact. Moreover, there is increasing evidence that many Southeast Asians – particularly those in Muslim-majority countries – judge the United States as much for its policies outside the region (Iraq, the Israeli-Palestinian conflict and, potentially, Iran) as for its actions in Southeast Asia.

U.S. policy toward ASEAN is not likely to alter that dynamic. To
be sure, the United States needs to expand and improve its much-
maligned "public diplomacy" policies in Southeast Asia, but
ASEAN may be too indirect a route.

A more serious and sustainable reason to increase U.S. involvement
with ASEAN lies in new trends in Asian regionalism. First, the
growing economic and financial nature of Asian regional architecture will eventually have an impact on American competitiveness,
if it is not already doing so. The proliferation of regional free trade
negotiations, as well as new currency regimes such as the Chiang
Mai Initiative, are moving economic policy toward the regional
and away from the bilateral arena.

Second, ASEAN and the ASEAN Regional Forum (ARF) are moving slowly and tentatively – but moving all the same – toward new
regional security arrangements. These new initiatives stay well
below the radar of the U.S. security umbrella in Asia, but early
positioning for the United States in this emerging dialogue may be
a wise investment. The ASEAN Concord II unveiled in Bali in
2003 proposed an ASEAN Security Community and urged a more
vigorous role for the group in the areas of peace-building, maritime
cooperation, among others. With Beijing's urging, ARF has established an annual defense ministers' meeting.

In broad terms, the United States supports the multilateralization
of security in the Asia-Pacific region and has contributed to this
trend as well. The annual U.S.-Thailand COBRA Gold exercises
have added new permanent partners and several more observer
nations. Even the over-reaching Regional Maritime Security
Initiative, which foundered when the littoral states of the
Malacca Straits were caught off guard, sparked joint maritime
patrols in the region.

However, beyond longstanding skepticism that ASEAN can become a more decisive and operational group, the United States must overcome some specific obstacles to expanding relations with ASEAN. First is the uneven quality of U.S. bilateral relations in Southeast Asia that would make it difficult for the United States to adopt a more uniform approach to the countries of the region. On the security side, for example, the United States has two treaty allies (Thailand and the Philippines); a group of strategic friends (Singapore, and increasingly Indonesia and Malaysia); and countries where the legacy of a past war requires that security cooperation proceed slowly and cautiously (Vietnam, Laos, and Cambodia).

Moreover, and perhaps more problematic, U.S. relations with Burma are not fully normal and, with the military regime's dismal response to the May 2008 cyclone and a controversial constitutional process, there seems to be little prospect for their immediate improvement. In recent years, proposals for high-profile U.S.-ASEAN summits have foundered on the issue of representation by Burma. It is too soon to determine whether recent events in Burma may weaken the regime's hold on power. Absent a dramatic improvement in the political situation there, however, U.S. policymakers will have to pick their way carefully through new policies that seem to expand U.S. ties with ASEAN, particularly those that require congressional approval.

A second constraint is current U.S. international trade policy, which makes it difficult for the United States to match the pace of new free trade agreement (FTA) arrangements in Southeast Asia. With the exception of the U.S.-Singapore FTA, even U.S. bilateral attempts to liberalize trade relations in the region have foundered. The U.S.-Thailand and U.S.-Malaysia FTA negotiations are seriously stalled, and it remains to be seen if new trade ministers in each country can resolve some of the domestic issues that have impeded progress. Nor is there a long queue of prospective new FTA bilateral agreements in the region. Vietnam has been mentioned informally as the next candidate. However, a dismal score on the FTA front does not mean that the United States has not made some progress in its trade relations with the region. The Trade and Investment Framework Agreements (TIFAs) with Vietnam and Indonesia were, in their own way, landmark agreements and could set the stage for FTAs at some point in the future.

That point may be several years away, however. Even if prospects were brighter in Southeast Asia, the United States would not be able to follow through on new trade agreements without a shift in the domestic political climate. International trade is clearly a flashpoint in the 2008 presidential campaign, and the campaigning Congress has not looked kindly upon recently signed FTA agreements. Moreover, it will be up to a new Congress to decide whether to renew the president's fast track authority, which would be an obvious aid, if not an outright necessity, in the negotiation of new agreements.

Recommendations and Conclusions

The current discourse on U.S. relations with ASEAN frequently portrays the United States as a passive actor, responding (or not) to regional developments and often lagging behind. A preliminary step toward deepening U.S. engagement with ASEAN would involve highlighting and extending current efforts from Washington.

First among these is the creation of the position of U.S. Ambassador for ASEAN Affairs, adopted this year by the State Department with strong initial encouragement from the Senate.

Although U.S. officials readily admit that the position is symbolic at this point, serious consideration should be given to its use as a springboard for further initiatives. The United States is the first regional power to establish such a position, and there are signs that other countries may follow suit, beginning with Japan. Moreover, some Southeast Asian governments are being urged to post their own ambassadors to ASEAN. This would ultimately create a virtual ASEAN diplomatic corps that would in itself be a new regional grouping and a potential coordinating mechanism.

Second is the March 2008 proposal by State Department Assistant Secretary of State Christopher Hill that the 2009 ARF meeting focus on developing a common regional disaster response plan. This would presumably build upon the international cooperation forged during the 2004 tsunami as well as the increasing tendency for joint exercises (COBRA Gold, Balikatan) to focus on humanitarian intervention. The Burma cyclone has made this recommendation sadly prescient, but it also underscores its timeliness and utility. The United States should move preliminary discussion of this initiative up to this summer's ARF meeting, to enable ASEAN and its partners to work toward implementation sooner. If a regional response mechanism is only marginally more acceptable than a Western-led international effort, as the Burmese government seemed to have signaled, thousands of lives might still be saved.

Lastly, the United States could reap exponential rewards by increasing its support for ASEAN's structures and projects that work with the region's civil societies. The "people's assembly" movement in ASEAN is in its infant stages, but this channel offers alternative routes to promote political liberalization and address nontraditional transnational security threats. In addition, a people-first approach to ASEAN could in time be a useful instrument for U.S. public diplomacy in the region, mitigating the disadvantages mentioned above.

Tilting Toward TAC

In recent years, the willingness (or reluctance) of the United States to sign the ASEAN Treaty of Amity and Cooperation has become a litmus test for greater U.S. engagement with Southeast Asia. To mitigate problems the U.S. brings to its relations with ASEAN, signing the TAC is probably the best short-term measure available to improve relations with the region, and for that reason alone it is a step worth taking. A secondary, but still important, reason is to give the United States a seat at the table of the East Asia Summit. To date, EAS meetings have not produced major initiatives, but there is growing acknowledgment that the summit is a permanent fixture in the Asian regional framework.

To mitigate problems the U.S. brings to its relations with

ASEAN, signing the TAC is probably the best short-term

measure available to improve relations with the region, and

for that reason alone it is a step worth taking.

The U.S. security community has thus far opposed signing the TAC, fearing that its pledge to resolve disputes without force would constrain U.S. military power in Asia. However, this would not be the first time that the United States has signed a treaty with such a provision: the 1928 Kellogg-Briand Pact had a similar requirement. As in 1928, this language in the TAC could presumably be addressed with a notification of reservation. A greater obstacle would likely be congressional opposition to ratifying a treaty that includes Burma as a signatory. Even if the TAC were to join the long list of treaties the United States has signed but not ratified, there would be some tangible value in taking the first step.

In election years, most policy studies focus on an agenda for a new administration and Congress. Signing the TAC should be an early recommendation for the new president in 2009. However, just as President Clinton took the initiative to visit Vietnam in the last days of his administration, signing the TAC might well be a good step for a lame duck president. New leaders often resent such babies in baskets, but this infant might be welcomed as a short cut to improving U.S. relations with Southeast Asia.

---

[1] China's growing relationship with Southeast Asia and its impact on U.S. interests in the region are the subject of growing debate and deserving of in-depth examination. See, for example, Joshua Kurlantzick, *Charm Offensive: How China's Soft Power is Transforming the World* (Yale University Press, 2007) and Bronson Percival, *The Dragon Looks South: China and Southeast Asia in the New Century* (Praeger, 2007).

[2] These are essentially a commitment to the peaceful resolution of disputes; non-interference in the internal affairs of member states; and requiring consensus in the decision-making process.

[3] Russia has signed the TAC but at this point has only been granted observer status in the EAS. Some regional analysts believe this is because growing U.S.-Russian tensions make the EAS reluctant to admit Moscow unless Washington is also a member.

COUNTERING TERRORISM IN EAST ASIA

Bronson Percival

Issue: Many Asians believe that the U.S. preoccupation with countering terrorism has skewed U.S. foreign policy priorities and led to neglect of key relationships in East Asia. Is there a different approach that would be more effective in promoting common efforts against the terrorist threat while allowing U.S. leaders to devote more attention to other important trends and relationships?

Introduction

The Bush administration's post-9/11 preoccupation with countering international terrorism transformed U.S. foreign policy priorities. The terrorist threat temporarily raised Southeast Asia's profile, while simultaneously diminishing East Asia's overall priority in Washington. South Asia drew increased attention.

Viewing Asia through a counter-terrorism lens is problematic. If the borderlands that link the Middle East and South Asia are included in "Asia," the insurgency in Afghanistan and the terrorist safe haven in Pakistan crowd out consideration of the consequences of the war against terrorism for most of "Asia." Moreover, the remnants of al-Qaeda's links are to the Middle East and Europe – not to East Asia. This essay will address the consequences of Washington's preoccupation with terrorism for East Asia.

East Asians are skeptical of U.S. counter-terrorism policy. Their broad criticism of America's global war on terrorism often conflates three distinct elements of recent U.S. foreign policy: comparative neglect of East Asia, incompetence in the Middle East, and insensitive "one size fits all" global anti-terrorist policies in East Asia. The first criticism is valid, the second has less to do with terrorism than with insurgencies, and the third is factually incorrect.

East Asia Neglected

Neither Asians nor the U.S. policy community were prepared for the sudden shift in U.S. foreign policy priorities as a consequence of the September 2001 al-Qaeda attacks in the United States. East Asia disappeared from center stage, and relations among major powers took a back seat to responding to a new threat from a non-state enemy. The subsequent discovery of terrorists in Southeast Asia led Washington to label that region the "second front" in the global war against terrorism, and brought new U.S. attention to a part of East Asia traditionally viewed as peripheral. Thus, in the view of many Asians, when the U.S. did pay attention, it focused on the wrong issue. In the view of some, it also focused on the wrong part of Asia. For those Asians and Americans convinced that China's growing economic and political influence poses the most important challenge and opportunity for Asia – and for the United States – Washington's post-9/11 priorities have been difficult to swallow.

Since September 2001, the United States has not ignored East Asia, but it has downgraded diplomatic relationships and kicked problems down the road. Stretched U.S. policymakers have focused on the North Korean nuclear problem and the construction of a strategic partnership with India. APEC meetings annually draw the president to East Asia, but the U.S. seems to have a tin ear for Asian concerns. The secretaries of state and defense have largely been absent. Congressional attention has been episodic and often focused on trade or human rights issues. An argument has been made that the U.S. has achieved "quiet victories" on trade liberalization and the promotion of democracy in Asia, but U.S. influence is fading.

Benign neglect, even indifference, is not the only explanation for fading influence. It is not clear that more attention would significantly alter fundamental trends. Beijing has supported U.S. counter-terrorism policies, profited from U.S. distraction in the Middle East, and steadily implemented its comprehensive campaign to increase China's economic and political influence with its neighbors. Japan and much of Southeast Asia may miss the patronage they have come to expect from the United States, but neither would support U.S. initiatives to contain China or constrain growing economic linkages in the region.

One consequence of U.S. neglect is that Asians pay less attention to Washington as they race ahead with constructing their own regional architecture and integrating their economies. A second is, with the exception of India, increasing anti-Americanism. Nonetheless, the United States maintains good relations with most East Asian states and remains a key player with considerable influence, if it is prepared to use it.

America Stumbles in the Middle East

East Asian elites do not accept the Bush administration's claim that the war in Iraq should be regarded as an integral part of the larger war on terrorism (the exception is former Singapore Prime

Minister Lee Kuan Yew). Iraq has not only diverted attention and resources from Asia, but also saddled Washington with a reputation for incompetence among many Asian elites. Polling data consistently demonstrates that it has also badly tarnished the U.S. image among Asian publics.

Asians share a widespread unease with the implications of a U.S.-led invasion of a sovereign country without U.N. sanction, the failure to discover weapons of mass destruction (WMD) in Iraq, the Abu Graib torture scandal, and the detention of terrorist suspects beyond the reach of U.S. courts, most notably at Guantanamo Bay. Moreover, declining U.S. credibility and moral leadership stokes already rising confidence, as well as nationalism, in Asia.

For much of Asia, counter-terrorism is seen as diverting the United States from its proper function, as a market and as a potential hedge should China revert to bullying. In Southeast Asia, the insurgencies in Iraq, the Palestinian territories, and, to a lesser extent, Afghanistan, continue to fan the flames of anti-Americanism among the region's 230 million Muslims. For this region's Muslims, the fundamental complaint against the U.S. involves not its policies in Asia, but the perceived assault by the United States and its allies on Muslims elsewhere.

Terrorism and Insurgencies in Asia: An Untold Story

In Asia, China worries about links between al-Qaeda and a few groups that seek independence for Xinjiang, one of which has been designated a terrorist organization by the United Nations. Beijing claims to have blocked at least two attempted terrorist attacks inside China, and is concerned about the threat of terrorist attacks outside the country in connection with the 2008 Olympic Games.

India has suffered a number of bloody terrorist attacks over the past several years. New Delhi has usually blamed external terrorist groups based in Pakistan and Bangladesh. The most recent attack, in the city of Jaipur, may be tied to a Bangladeshi militant group. These are serious threats, but they are not comparable to the threat once faced by Southeast Asia. Al-Qaeda had penetrated Southeast Asia — which was temporarily labeled, for good reasons, the second front in the war on terrorism.

Southeast Asian elites, who have complained for decades about Washington's neglect, often react to renewed U.S. attention by grumbling about insensitivity to regional conditions in countering terrorism. In fact, the United States tailored its regional policy to de-emphasize military responses, stress cooperation to capture al-Qaeda-linked terrorists, and leave regional Islamic terrorists and insurgents to Southeast Asians. Southeast Asia provides a case study of how the U.S. should think again about its confrontation with Islamic terrorists.

In Southeast Asia, the United States designed and implemented a low-cost, low-profile effort based on cooperation with key regional states. It did so for several reasons. First, the region was not considered so close to the heart of the U.S. anti-terrorism campaign as to require a large military response, as in Afghanistan and Iraq; but not so secondary that transnational terrorism could be ignored. Second, Washington largely distinguished between al-Qaeda and its regional ally, the Jema'ah Islamiyah, and local minority Muslim insurgencies. Third, resources were already stretched and the United States wanted to focus on and quickly cut international terrorists' links. Fourth, a few senior U.S. government officials understood that Indonesia was at the heart of the problem and recognized that direct action to capture terrorists would prove counterproductive.

When international terrorists were discovered in Southeast Asia in 2002, Washington faced three problems. First, the United States and regional states needed to sort out a division of labor. The United States did not want to be dragged into local conflicts, but several Southeast Asian governments sought anti-terrorism assistance on their terms and increased economic assistance. Second, Southeast Asian elites insisted they did not want the United States to see the region purely through a terrorism lens, but also worried about Washington's long-term commitment to the region. Third, for Indonesia, which was recovering from the Asian financial crisis during a chaotic transition to democracy, terrorism ranked low as a national priority. Moreover, the Indonesian government at the time was in a state of denial about terrorism, only finally broken after a series of costly bombings in Bali, Jakarta, and elsewhere in the archipelago.

At the cost of a couple hundred million dollars annually, the United States provided training and other assistance, encouraged intelligence exchanges among Southeast Asian countries, limited its military footprint, initiated a rare resort to multilateralism with the Association of Southeast Asian Nations (ASEAN) and Asia-Pacific Economic Cooperation (APEC) to provide political cover for cooperation, and tailored its policies and programs for each country.

Singapore immediately identified terrorism as an existential threat, and opportunism and access to U.S. assistance brought the Philippines on board. The U.S. military footprint was confined to advisors to the Filipino military in their campaign against thugs with an Islamic gloss; while pressure to take on the major representative of Muslim minorities, the Moro Islamic Liberation Front, was resisted. Washington and Bangkok agreed that the United States had no role to play in confronting the brutal Malay insurgency in southern Thailand. Despite some tensions, the United

States played a quiet, secondary role in Malaysia's detention of terrorists. After highlighting the issue of maritime security, the United States left the lead to regional states while quietly providing substantial assistance.

From 2002 to 2004, Indonesian political elites competed for the support of Islamic extremists and refused to detain, capture, or try most Jema'ah Islamiyah terrorists, while other Indonesians worried that counter-terrorism would be used to undermine hard-won protections for human rights and democracy. This presented a dilemma for Washington, which resisted the temptation to overreact. The election of a new Indonesian president in 2004 and improved police capabilities allowed Indonesia to adopt its own approach to counter-terrorism. The courts have tried and jailed hundreds of terrorists, and undermined their legitimacy in the eyes of Indonesians.

The result is that al-Qaeda no longer has a presence in Southeast Asia; its regional ally has been badly wounded and much of it is turning away from violence. The United States continues to provide low-profile assistance. However, once international terrorists' links were severed, senior policy officials and the media forgot about a marginal area in the global war against terrorism. Instead of trumpeting successful cooperation with partners, based on separating international terrorism from local insurgencies, Washington has moved on.

Recommendations and Conclusions

There are no magic solutions to the problems of perceived neglect of East Asia and of perceived American flailing in the Middle East. Securing support for the next phase in the war against terrorism will be difficult because, with a few exceptions, East Asians don't believe they are now directly threatened. The most effective steps the United States could take have less to do with U.S. policy in Asia than with U.S. actions in the Middle East. No East Asian government will provide significant help in extricating the United States from Iraq, but a major reduction in U.S. forces or in violence in Iraq would improve the U.S. image.

The most effective steps the United States could take have less to do with U.S. policy in Asia than with U.S. actions in the Middle East. No East Asian government will provide significant help in extricating the United States from Iraq, but a major reduction in U.S. forces or in violence in Iraq would improve the U.S. image.

In addition, the next administration should consider the following three points on terrorism as it seeks to restore America's reputation and revive U.S. influence in East Asia.

First, Washington should not demand assistance from East Asian governments that they will not provide, or will only provide under extreme pressure. Such demands are counterproductive in the long run.

Second, don't preach in East Asia. In revamping U.S. public diplomacy to redress the deterioration in public support, the United

States should not shy away from discussing terrorism, but instead stress our understanding of the local context and reliance on regional partners. Our cooperation with Southeast Asian partners provides a good example of an effective counter-terrorism strategy, and we should praise Southeast Asians for their success.

Third, Washington no longer proclaims that it is engaged in a global war against terrorism, but still tends to perpetuate the image of a global jihad. However, the threat now includes a host of increasingly scattered regional and local insurgencies and terrorist groups. The United States needs to further adjust its thinking and its message. As we seek to shift the burden for dealing with Islamic violence associated with regional and local terrorists and long-standing insurgencies to regional states, while we concentrate on the remaining international terrorist groups now based outside of East Asia; we should examine our experience in Southeast Asia to determine whether there are lessons that can be applied elsewhere in the continuing campaign against terrorism.

U.S.-INDIA RELATIONS

Karl F. Inderfurth

Issue: U.S. relations with India have improved dramatically over the last decade, as symbolized by the efforts by the two governments over the past two years to conclude an agreement on civil nuclear cooperation. India is both an important country in its own right and a potential counterweight to China's growing wealth and power, even while India's non-aligned tradition retains deep roots in Indian society. Can the U.S.-Indian relationship be strengthened without assuming an anti-China character? Should a new U.S. administration seek a strategic partnership with India, and if so how?

Introduction

On March 27, 2008, five former U.S. secretaries of state – Henry Kissinger, James Baker, Warren Christopher, Madeleine Albright, and Colin Powell – took part in a roundtable discussion entitled, "Bipartisan Advice to the Next Administration." During their conversation, this question was posed: "What should a new administration do in terms of dealing with India?"

Former Secretary Kissinger responded: "The relationship with India is one of the very positive things that is happening. We can cooperate with them both on ideological grounds and on strategic grounds. It's one of the positive legacies that the new administration will inherit."

After decades of being "estranged democracies," the United States and India have entered a new era that can best be described as "engaged democracies." As former Under Secretary of State for Political Affairs Nicholas Burns has written:

> *The United States and India have quietly forged the strongest relationship the two countries have enjoyed since India's independence in 1947. For most of the past 60 years, the Cold War and vastly differing ideological and governing philosophies kept us, at best, fitful partners. That all began to change a decade ago, when President Bill Clinton's efforts led to the first great opening in our relations. In 2001 President Bush launched an even more ambitious drive, culminating in impressive agreements regarding civilian nuclear power, trade, science and agriculture with India's reformist prime minister, Manmohan Singh.*[1]

Burns added that with the rapid pace of progress between Washington and New Delhi and the potential benefits to American interests so substantial, "within a generation Americans may view India as one of our two or three most important strategic partners." India's Ambassador to the United States, Ronen Sen, agrees this is the direction the two countries are heading in: "The relationship has been qualitatively transformed into what can be truly called a strategic partnership. By 'strategic,' I mean it's not based on any transient considerations, but on long-term national interests of both countries converging."

Emerging India

In its 2004 report entitled, "Mapping the Global Future," the National Intelligence Council (NIC) predicted the emergence of

India and China as new major global powers in the 21st century. According to the NIC, their emergence — "similar to the rise of Germany in the 19th century and the United States in the early 20th century — will transform the geopolitical landscape, with impacts potentially as dramatic as those of the previous two centuries. A combination of sustained high economic growth, expanding military capabilities, and large populations will be at the root of the expected rapid rise in economic and political power for both countries."

India's economic performance in recent years has been especially remarkable. With its economic growth rates at 9 percent and 9.4 percent the last two fiscal years, India now has the third largest economy in the world in purchasing power parity terms. The country's gross domestic product (GDP) has crossed the trillion-dollar mark for the first time in history, joining the world's elite 11-member nation Trillionaires Club. Its thriving information technology (IT) sector has some of the largest and best known IT firms in the world. General Motors' CEO says India will soon emerge as the second-largest auto market in the world. In sum, as *The Economist* put it, "the question is no longer whether India can fly, but how high."

The country's gross domestic product (GDP) has crossed the trillion-dollar mark for the first time in history, joining the world's elite 11-member nation Trillionaires Club.

That same question can also be posed about what the future holds in store for U.S.-India relations.

Recommendations and Conclusions

Assuming the next U.S. president who takes office on January 20, 2009 views India in the same emerging global power context as the last two administrations – as is highly likely given the strong bipartisan support for improved U.S.-India relations – how should the new administration proceed to expand this new strategic partnership? Clearly that effort should be broad-based, befitting the range of bilateral, regional, and global interests shared by the two countries. Moreover, it should be ambitious, building on the foundation laid over the past several years. The following seven point agenda should therefore be considered.

1. Strengthen Strategic Ties

Many Americans understand the growing strategic importance of India. A strong India is important for balance of power purposes in Asia and for providing stability in the volatile and strategically important Indian Ocean littoral area.

A strong India is important for balance of power purposes in Asia and for providing stability in the volatile and strategically important Indian Ocean littoral area.

A cursory look at a map underscores the potential strategic importance of India. Jutting down 1,500 miles into the middle of the

Indian Ocean, India is in a position to safeguard sea lanes that are used to transport more than half the world's oil and gas. The navies of the United States and India have begun to conduct joint exercises aimed against piracy, terrorism, and any other threats to maritime commerce.

There has been a quantum jump in U.S.-India defense ties in the past several years — with joint military exercises, the signing of a 10-year defense framework agreement, and increased interest in defense procurement and collaboration between defense industries. In March, Defense Secretary Gates led a 50-member delegation of defense and business experts to New Delhi and spoke of an increased arms trade between the two countries, as well as an increased flow of high technology from the United States to India. Of special interest is Lockheed Martin and Boeing's bid to build 126 jet fighters for the Indian Air Force, a contract that could be worth $10 billion dollars.

Another arena for greater strategic cooperation is in counter-terrorism. India has been a target of terrorist attacks longer than the United States. Expanding counter-terrorism cooperation requires increased information sharing and building tighter liaison bonds with India's intelligence and security services. Closer U.S.-India intelligence ties began with the establishment of a Joint Counter-Terrorism Working Group during the Clinton administration and have been accelerated by the Bush administration post-9/11.

Influential Indians such as K. Subrahmanyan also believe that increased U.S.-Indian security ties — broadly defined — make sense: "The U.S. and India have a convergence in terms of the central security challenges they will face in the future, such as terrorism; proliferation of chemical, biological and nuclear technologies; international crime; narcotics; HIV/AIDS; and climate change."

2. Realize Economic Potential

Underpinning the strategic partnership should be a concerted effort to realize the full economic potential of the U.S.-India relationship. Steps need to be taken to deepen commercial ties, identify and remove impediments on both sides (still far too many), and clear the way for a new era of trade cooperation. Innovative mechanisms like the CEO forum are also key drivers of the economic relationship, as it has brought to the table 20 top Indian and American chief executive officers representing more than a trillion dollars of capital.

Deeper economic ties will also have the added advantage of providing needed ballast in the overall relationship when political differences arise, as they surely will. A current example is Washington's effort to isolate Tehran, including opposition to the proposed Iran-Pakistan-India gas pipeline; and New Delhi's determination to remain engaged with the Islamic Republic.

While trade in goods and services between the United States and India has been expanding — bilateral trade is growing over 20 percent per year — India ranked only 19th in 2006 among U.S. trading partners, well below the capacity of the two large economies. Two-way trade amounted to $31 billion dollars. By contrast, U.S.-China trade was 10 times that amount. Foreign Direct Investment (FDI) tells the same story. Overall, India's share of global foreign investment remains very low at less than 1 percent.

India is taking steps to attract more foreign investment. Officials have set a target of $30 billion, more than doubling the last financial year's total. Of particular interest is infrastructure investment – including the development of power grids, ports and highways, and communications networks – which are all critical to sustaining India's high rate of economic growth.

While trade in goods and services between the United States and India has been expanding — bilateral trade is growing over 20 percent per year — India ranked only 19th in 2006 among U.S. trading partners, well below the capacity of the two large economies.

In addition, U.S. and Indian officials have set a goal of doubling bilateral trade over the next three years. It is time to accelerate the growth in these ties. The benefits flow both ways, as was evidenced in the conclusion last year of a longstanding market access dispute. Eighteen years since the initial Indian request, the first consignment of Indian mangoes shipped from Mumbai arrived in the United States, opening up the world's largest market for mangoes to the world's biggest producer of mangoes. The Indian commerce minister said the shipment was "a major breakthrough that augurs well" for Indian agricultural exports. More such breakthroughs are needed to realize the full potential of the U.S.-India economic relationship.

3. Pursue a Broader Nuclear Dialogue

It has long been a goal of the United States to engage India as a partner in global efforts to control the spread of nuclear weapons. But for more than a quarter of a century, the two countries have been on the opposite side of the nuclear divide – unable to reconcile India's nuclear weapons program and its security compulsions with the nuclear nonproliferation concerns and policies of the United States.

The U.S.-India civilian nuclear agreement announced by President Bush and Prime Minister Singh in July 2005 launched a major effort to bridge that divide. Mohammad El Baradei — the head of the International Atomic Energy Agency – announced his support, calling the agreement "a milestone, timely for ongoing efforts to consolidate the non-proliferation regime, combat nuclear terrorism, and strengthen nuclear safety."

But almost three years later, and after the U.S. Congress overwhelming approved implementing legislation, the prospects for concluding the agreement before the Bush administration leaves office are fading. Most recently, it has run into stiff opposition from members of the leftist parties in India's ruling coalition who are strongly opposed to any suggestion of outside interference in India's internal affairs, especially by the United States. This is a longstanding point of contention within the Indian body politic that will have to be taken into account as the two countries address other sensitive political issues, even as the level of confidence and trust between the two countries and their official and private-sector representatives continues to grow.

Still, with the announcement of the agreement, the United States has explicitly recognized India's status as a full-fledged nuclear power, and commits itself to a partnership in the realm of civilian nuclear energy. Over time that may open the door to an even broader nuclear dialogue the United States and India could pursue, one that is attracting increasing international attention.

In an important article first published in January 2006 entitled, "A World Free of Nuclear Weapons," former high-ranking U.S. officials George Shultz, William Perry, Henry Kissinger, and Sam Nunn argue that the world is entering a new nuclear era, more dangerous than before, with nuclear know-how proliferating and non-state terrorist groups seeking to obtain and use weapons of mass destruction. They argue that a bold new vision is needed by the international community to reverse this trend. They cite a former American president and Indian prime minister as inspiration for their declared goal of a "nuclear free world": Ronald Reagan and Rajiv Gandhi.

The United States and India should pursue this new nuclear dialogue with or without finalizing the civilian nuclear agreement — but it will have more credibility if that deal is consummated.

The United States and India should pursue this new nuclear dialogue with or without finalizing the civilian nuclear agreement — but it will have more credibility if that deal is consummated. At the same time, it is also essential to recognize that the civilian nuclear agreement is an important part – but not the sum total – of the much improved and expanding broad-based relationship between the two countries that already includes sensitive areas once virtually off limits to any form of cooperation, such as high technology transfers and joint ventures in space. Indeed, India will soon launch its first unmanned mission to the moon. Chandrayaan I will carry two American NASA payloads.

4. Highlight Higher Education

A 2005 policy report by a high-level panel of U.S. and Indian experts states: "Higher education is among the most important, and least appreciated, foundations of the budding partnership between India and the United States." (Report of the Joint Task Force of Pacific Council on International Policy and Observer Research Foundation, "India-US Relations: A Vision for the Future"). The report further says that India has the capacity to become a knowledge producer rather than a supplier of talent, that it should aspire to become an education hub for the region, and that American universities and research institutions could aid that process through joint ventures and collaborative efforts with Indian academic institutions.

The benefits for India of higher education collaboration with the United States are many: increasing the quality of its higher education opportunities, retaining good talent within the country, and reaping the benefits of foreign investment.

The benefits for India of higher education collaboration with the United States are many: increasing the quality of its higher education opportunities, retaining good talent within the country, and reaping the benefits of foreign investment. For the United States, there will be greater opportunities for exchanges and to learn and collaborate in fields of increasing importance to both countries — including science, public health, and information technology.

5. Support India's United Nations Bid

Enhanced U.S.-India cooperation should also extend to the institutions of global governance. Here the United States is missing an excellent opportunity to do what the Bush administration has said is its goal: "To help India become a major power in the 21st century." It is time for the United States to publicly support India's bid for a permanent seat on the UN Security Council and to work actively with India (and others) to accomplish the goal of Security Council expansion. With its thriving democracy, its billion plus population, its expanding economy, and its longstanding contributions to UN peacekeeping, the case for a permanent Indian seat has never been stronger.

It is time for the United States to publicly support India's bid for a permanent seat on the UN Security Council and to work actively with India (and others) to accomplish the goal of Security Council expansion.

6. Collaborate in the Neighborhood

Another area for greater collaboration should be at the regional level, in the subcontinent itself. Both India and the United States want a South Asia that is prosperous, stable and democratic. Already, the United States and India are working together in Nepal as it pursues a permanent peace and a new political dispensation. India and the United States should also cooperate in trying to stabilize Sri Lanka and Bangladesh, both of which face significant internal political difficulties.

India and the United States have a shared interest in a secure and stable Afghanistan. India's leaders are rightly alarmed at the resurgence of the Taliban since 2005 and the regeneration of al-Qaeda and other extremist elements in the tribal areas along the Afghanistan-Pakistan border. New Delhi is prepared to do more to help in Afghanistan and should be encouraged by the United States and the United Nations to do so. One obstacle, however, is finding a way to overcome Pakistan's suspicions of India's involvement in Afghanistan, and vice-versa.

The toughest longstanding issue in the South Asia neighborhood remains India's relations with Pakistan and attempts to advance the nascent Indo-Pakistani dialogue. In recent years, this dialogue has produced some practical steps on normalizing ties and confidence building measures; and the two sides are now engaged in perhaps their most serious exploration of the underlying source of friction: the Kashmir conflict. With the establishment of a new democratically elected civilian government in Pakistan, the two countries resumed their "composite dialogue" in May when India's External Affairs Minister, Pranab Mukherjee, traveled to Islamabad to meet with his new counterpart, Foreign Minister Shad Mehmood Qureshi. The United States should signal its strong support for

India and Pakistan as they seek to improve their relations and resolve their differences, but should defer to them as they grapple with the best approach on how to accomplish this.

The United States should signal its strong support for India and Pakistan as they seek to improve their relations and resolve their differences, but should defer to them as they grapple with the best approach on how to accomplish this.

---

7. Promote a Cooperative Triangle

Along with the much-improved U.S.-India relationship has come questions about the underlying motivations for this new direction in American foreign policy, specifically whether it represents a hedge by Washington against a rising China – India's most consequential neighbor and, as of 2006, India's largest trading partner.

Indeed there are geopolitical thinkers in each capital who seek improved relations against the third party. Some in Beijing and New Delhi see strengthened Sino-Indian ties as a constraint on American hegemony. Others in Washington and New Delhi are suspicious of China and seek to build U.S.-India relations (particularly military ties) as a strategic counterweight to growing Chinese power.

These manipulative temptations should be resisted. Strengthened U.S. ties with India have their own strategic logic and imperatives and should not be part of a China containment strategy, something Indian officials would strongly oppose. On his March visit to New Delhi, Defense Secretary Gates attempted to assuage Indian concerns in this regard, especially as they relate to growing U.S.-India military ties:

"I don't see our improving military relationship in this region in the context of any other country, including China. When you look at the kinds of activities that we are engaged in and the kind of exercises that we conduct…these expanding relationships don't necessarily have to be directed against anybody."[2]

Strengthened U.S. ties with India have their own strategic logic and imperatives and should not be part of a China containment strategy, something Indian officials would strongly oppose.

While a new interactive dynamic has begun between the United States and Asia's two continental powers, the task for all three is to manage ties as a cooperative – not a competitive – triangle. One way to further a closer, cooperative relationship between the United States (and the leading industrialized nations) and India and China would be to make these two global powers formal members of an expanded Group of Eight. As former UN Ambassador Richard Holbrooke has noted, G-8 initiatives on energy, climate change, AIDS, Africa, and poverty will have little effect without China and India.

Two critical issues that the three countries should address are energy and the environment. The United States and China are the world's two largest importers of energy. India is the world's sixth largest consumer of energy resources. With an energy competition looming, India and China have signed an agreement to promote collaboration between their enterprises, including joint exploration and development of hydrocarbon resources in third countries. This is an initiative the United States should encourage: the growing interdependence of the United States, China, and India, including in the vital area of energy and its environmental consequences, will only increase in coming years. So will demands from the international community for all three countries to become full participants in dealing with the dangers posed by climate change and global warming.

As former UN ambassador Richard Holbrooke has noted, G-8

initiatives on energy, climate change, AIDS, Africa, and poverty

will have little effect without China and India.

Another issue on which India, the United States and China are uniquely poised to cooperate is international health. India and China have two of the world's largest populations of HIV-infected people; both have had experience with avian influenza; China was the original home to severe acute respiratory syndrome (SARS). At the same time, both countries have large pools of trained manpower. The United States has scientific links with both. With greater transparency and an international cooperative mechanism, they could become invaluable resources for dealing with deadly global epidemics.

The growing interdependence of the United States, China,

and India, including in the vital area of energy and its

environmental consequences, will only increase in coming years.

Recommendations and Conclusions

The National Intelligence Council's 2004 report predicting India's rise as a "new major global power" in the 21st century has raised expectations for that country's long-term prospects. But the NIC also called attention to several factors that could impede India's emergence as a major global player:

> While India has clearly evolved beyond what the Indians themselves referred to as the 2-3 percent 'Hindu growth rate,' the legacy of a stifling bureaucracy still remains. The country is not yet attractive for foreign investment and faces strong political challenges as it continues down the path of economic reform. In many other respects, India still resembles other developing states in the problems it must overcome, including the large numbers, particularly in rural areas, who have not enjoyed the major benefits from economic growth.

As the United States pursues its policy of greater engagement with India, these factors should not be overlooked. At the same time, it is clear that a new era has begun for U.S.-India relations, one that, not long ago, only a few individuals could imagine.

One of those was Chester Bowles, a distinguished former American ambassador to India, who lamented in a 1969 interview that one U.S. administration after another "ignored a major nation which is going to have in the future a very big impact on the world. But I was never able to persuade the White House and the State Department of its key importance." The late Ambassador Bowles can now "rest in peace" because the White House and State Department finally have recognized India's significance. The last two American presidents – Clinton and Bush – recognized that fundamental change was under way with India as an emerging global power and acted accordingly. A strong foundation for a vibrant U.S.-India relationship has been established, upon which the next U.S. administration can build.

---

[1] "Heady Times for India and the U.S.," *Washington Post,* April 29, 2007.

[2] "US-India Hi-Tech Trade Set to Zoom," *Indian Abroad,* March 7, 2008.

PAKISTAN: OLD PROBLEMS, NEW ANSWERS?

Teresita C. Schaffer

Issue: Despite substantial domestic opposition, Pakistan's Musharraf government provided and continues to provide invaluable support to the United States in its intervention in Afghanistan. At the same time, Pakistan's military-dominated government and the nexus between Pakistan's military and radical Islamic groups inside that country are glaringly in contradiction with U.S. political values and counter-terrorism interests. How should a new U.S. administration address these policy anomalies?

Introduction

The fundamental forces that have made Pakistan central to U.S. strategic interests will carry on into the next administration and beyond. The United States needs to deal with two urgent problems: the impact of a porous border on instability and terrorism in Afghanistan, and domestic insurgency in Pakistan. It must also support the health of Pakistan's democracy, its weak institutions, and the economy. These long-term issues will undermine progress on counter-terrorism if not attended to. The time is not ripe for an India-Pakistan initiative, but the United States needs to have an active "watching brief" on that difficult relationship.

The United States has had a roller-coaster relationship with Pakistan, with periods of intense collaboration ending in abrupt cutoffs. The closest ties have come during periods of military rule.

This includes the years since 9/11 — marked by close collaboration, good military ties, and high aid flows, but also growing resentment. Many Pakistanis blame the United States for hypocritical lip-service to democracy and for sucking Pakistan into "America's war" in Afghanistan and its spillover in Pakistan. Anti-Americanism is at record highs, and many Pakistanis have been wondering when the next U.S.-Pakistan "divorce" is going to occur.

Pakistan is struggling through the transition to an elected government. The United States had personalized its relationship to President Musharraf and, until the last few months before the February 2008 elections, gave little support to restoration of democracy. Pakistan's voters rejected Musharraf's party, but he remained president. If we want Pakistan to have a reasonably orderly government and to sustain policies that advance regional peace, then democracy and civilian institutions need to become stronger. The internal contradictions in a government composed of two parties that mistrust one another make this a difficult job. The collective paranoia about the United States will require us to act with extraordinary discretion.

The Pakistan-Afghanistan Nexus: Borders and Insurgencies

At the same time, the United States has invested heavily in building a new Afghanistan, and is looking to increase its troop strength there. Controlling the porous border must remain a major focus of U.S. policy. The new Pakistani government, like the Musharraf government, will want to continue this effort. But success in border management is impossible without tackling the much deeper problems on both sides of the border.

Pakistanis would like to have a stable neighbor in Afghanistan, but are increasingly skeptical that the current Afghan government is capable of integrating the provinces bordering Pakistan into the rather rudimentary polity that is the Afghan state. Pakistan's elected government has tried to put Pakistan-Afghanistan relations on a better footing, but it is too early to say how well they have succeeded.

Pakistanis would like to have a stable neighbor in Afghanistan, but are increasingly skeptical that the current Afghan government is capable of integrating the provinces bordering Pakistan into the rather rudimentary polity that is the Afghan state.

Bad relations between Pakistan and Afghanistan are nothing new. What gives their discord such importance today is the support Afghan insurgents are receiving from within Pakistan. Afghans blame it on a cynical dual policy by Pakistan's intelligence services; others argue that it represents Pakistan's "plan B" in case Karzai's government proves incapable of exercising firmer and more constructive control. The Pakistan government hotly denies both contentions. Pakistan considers U.S. calls for Pakistan to "do more" about this problem unfair, considering the difficulty of the task and Afghanistan's inability to control its side of the border. From Washington's point of view, sanctuaries for Taliban leaders in Pakistan present a mortal danger to the possibility of a peaceful Afghanistan.

Bad relations between Pakistan and Afghanistan are nothing new. What gives their discord such importance today is the support Afghan insurgents are receiving from within Pakistan.

Border management leads directly to the most contentious issues in Pakistan's domestic politics. The Pakistan-Afghanistan border runs along the parts of Pakistan that are the least well integrated into the Pakistani state, including the province of Balochistan – where insurgency has flourished off and on for more than 30 years – and the Federally Administered Tribal Areas, which have been largely ungoverned for at least a couple of centuries. The leadership of Afghanistan's Taliban movement goes to Balochistan for R&R; Pakistan's counterpart of the Taliban movement has a kind of headquarters in the tribal areas.

As Pakistan has tried to bring both areas under tighter control, a new and more acute insurgency has flared up, sparking trouble not just in these border areas but in the "settled areas" of the country. The dividing line between the Pakistani Taliban and their Afghan counterparts is blurry. Pakistanis across the political spectrum recognize that the insurgency is a mortal threat to the authority of the state. The year 2007 saw more than 1,300 people killed in militant attacks. Suicide bombings claimed some 270 lives in the first three months of 2008, most of them in attacks on military personnel or installations. The army moved into the enormous Red Mosque complex in central Islamabad in July 2007, after its radical leadership and students amassed a large cache of arms and began conducting "raids" and kidnapping people off the capital's streets. The operation left well over 100 people dead. A radical cleric and his vigilantes held several towns in the Swat Valley last year. While the army reclaimed some of this territory, the test of wills is far from over.

Making Policy in an Uneasy Coalition

This was the situation that the newly elected Pakistani government inherited when it took office in early March. The issues of reducing the powers of the presidency and restoring the judges Musharraf had fired in 2007 soon became a proxy for their ability to keep the coalition together. After several crises, the second-largest party, the Muslim League of former Prime Minister Nawaz Sharif, pulled out of the Cabinet on May 13, 2008, promising to continue to support the government. Musharraf's presence as president tends to push the coalition together, at least for the time being. As long as the coalition holds, Musharraf's power will be limited. But there will be further crises, and Musharraf will surely be looking for an opportunity to move back to center stage if the elected leaders are discredited.

The one issue on which the government has tried to act is the insurgency. Like the problems of the judiciary and of presidential powers, it is a tightrope walk – but this time, the United States is deeply involved. "The war on terror" is now seen as synonymous with "America's War" – and with Musharraf. A government whose principal members ran as "the un-Musharraf" recognizes that it must find a more effective way to end the domestic insurgency. But in doing so, it needs to establish its credibility as an independent actor, and must show that its policy is different from those of Musharraf and of Washington.

"The war on terror" is now seen as synonymous with

"America's War" — and with Musharraf.

The new government's efforts stressed political negotiations rather than military action. The lead role in the negotiations went to the newly elected Chief Minister of the Northwest Frontier Province, representing the Awami National Party, long the voice of Pashtun nationalism and a resolutely secular party. The government concluded a cease-fire with the leader of the Pakistani Taliban. The jury is still out on this effort. Suicide bombings stopped for five weeks in late March and April 2008, which was much welcomed in Pakistan, but a couple more took place in May and, on June 2, a car bomb hit the Danish Embassy in Islamabad. Not surprisingly, the emphasis on negotiation is causing deep uneasiness in the U.S. government. In fact, political negotiation is not new. Musharraf's deal in Waziristan, part of the Tribal Areas, ended badly, like the military intervention that preceded it.

Economics and Institutions

Despite its need to avoid over-identification with Washington, the new Pakistani government wants to keep the United States engaged. It does not want to lose U.S. economic and military assistance. Both it and the army want to enhance the military's counter-insurgency capacity, a high priority for the United States military.

Despite its need to avoid over-identification with

Washington, the new Pakistani government wants to keep

the United States engaged. It does not want to lose U.S.

economic and military assistance.

Looking further ahead, Pakistan's high economic growth of the past few years conceals an inadequate level of investment, both in the Pakistani people and their productive capacity. Pakistan's food and electricity crises, which erupted during the election campaign, need tending. Sustaining growth will require job creation as well as a major jump in health and education.

The second long-term issue is the weakness of Pakistan's civilian institutions. Pakistan has spent over half its independent life under military-led regimes. The army remains by far its strongest institution, and it expects to have the dominant say on all aspects of national policy that touch on security, including relations with Pakistan's immediate neighbors and with the United States. Civilian institutions have not prospered. Pakistan's major political parties are family-dominated; the judiciary has been intimidated by both military and civilian governments; and the institutions that make government work – revenue collection, policing, civil service, and others – are widely regarded as not up to the challenges they face. Fixing these institutions is a long-term challenge for Pakistan. The United States cannot do the job, but needs to play a supporting rather than obstructing role.

Civilian institutions have not prospered. Pakistan's major

political parties are family-dominated; the judiciary has been

intimidated by both military and civilian governments; and

the institutions that make government work — revenue collection,

policing, civil service, and others — are widely regarded as not

up to the challenges they face.

If the elected government survives its internal contradictions, this may be a moment when Pakistan is more amenable than usual to institutional change. Musharraf's final year before the elected government took power revolved around his efforts to regain control of the judiciary. The issue of judicial independence has popular steam behind it, and there may be an opportunity to strengthen rule of law despite the questionable track record of several of Pakistan's current political leaders. The army appears inclined to take something of a sabbatical from direct involvement in politics. If the country's institutions of civilian government can make a fresh start, they may be more successful in the future in balancing civilian against military needs.

Recommendations and Conclusions

Many of the interests that drive U.S. policy will remain substantially the same, but the experience of the past seven years and the changed circumstances in Pakistan argue for some fresh thinking about how best to achieve them. Three elements are key:

First, both border management and the long-term U.S. relationship with Pakistan argue for strong connections with the Pakistan military. The primary channel for this should be the U.S. military, however: the United States has no interest in encouraging new political ambitions on the part of the Pakistan military. Counterinsurgency training and professional contacts are important tools. In addition, a stepped-up effort at joint strategic planning including the United States, Afghanistan, and Pakistan is urgently needed for addressing Afghanistan's insurgency. This should ideally lead to an understanding on deployment of the foreign forces in Afghanistan so that they can reinforce Pakistan's efforts at border management from the other side of the border.

A stepped-up effort at joint strategic planning including the United States, Afghanistan, and Pakistan is urgently needed for addressing Afghanistan's insurgency.

Second, Senator Biden's proposal for a generous economic "democracy dividend" for Pakistan is attractive, but needs to be coupled with a strategic approach to Pakistan's economy. Energy price increases have already driven down the value of the rupee, and Pakistan's growth in the past few years has been very energy-intensive. The United States could help the resulting foreign exchange squeeze by liberalizing market access for Pakistan's textiles. The formidable political obstacles to textile liberalization might be manageable if the administration made the case that this was central to our anti-terrorism goals. Our aid program should focus on job creation and investment in Pakistan's people.

The United States could help the resulting foreign exchange

squeeze by liberalizing market access for Pakistan's textiles.

The formidable political obstacles to textile liberalization

might be manageable if the administration made the case that

this was central to our anti-terrorism goals.

Third, we must focus more on strengthening democracy and government institutions. This means doing everything possible to encourage the elected government to succeed, and working seriously with its leaders; but not portraying any particular individual as Washington's favorite. Economic assistance is part of this long-term support, as is public and technical assistance for the institutions on which any decent government in Pakistan will depend, including the judiciary.

The challenge for the United States will be to keep its eye on both the Afghanistan and insurgency problems and the long-term health of Pakistan's democratic institutions. We cannot ignore any of these. If Pakistan's elected government falls apart and is unable to manage a decent succession, the result will not be a return to the relatively orderly days of the "old Musharraf." Rather, it is likely to lead to an authoritarian regime presiding over massive social discontent – not a recipe for an improved policy environment.

The challenge for the United States will be to keep its eye on both the Afghanistan and insurgency problems and the long-term health of Pakistan's democratic institutions. We cannot ignore any of these.

Other U.S. policies that go beyond Pakistan will also be important. While the time does not seem right for a major initiative on India-Pakistan diplomacy, Washington needs to keep an eye on that peace process, and if possible work to avoid the kind of sudden crisis that has occurred in the past. And the overall success of U.S. policy in Pakistan will hinge on the United States' ability to change the widespread perception that U.S. policy in recent years has become anti-Muslim.

Putting this new approach in place should not wait for the new administration. Things are moving fast in Pakistan. Reversing the trend toward insurgency and strengthening democracy is a national task, not one that should be linked with a particular administration. There is no time to lose.

U.S. POLICY TOWARD AFGHANISTAN

Theodore L. Eliot Jr.

Issue: History highlights the difficulties that foreign occupiers encounter in trying to stabilize the situation on the ground in Afghanistan. Given the scale of the U.S. commitment to Afghanistan, and the dire consequences that could result from a U.S. withdrawal, what conclusions should emerge from a policy review by the new U.S. administration of the U.S. involvement in Afghanistan? Are there different economic and social policies that could favorably alter the outlook?

Introduction

This paper examines the stakes for the United States in Afghanistan, the difficulties in protecting and promoting our interests there, and progress and setbacks since our invasion in late 2001. It concludes with specific policy recommendations for a new U.S. administration.

The road to a stable Afghanistan that can secure its own territory is long and arduous. Yet the United States and its partners in the United Nations and NATO must take that road or risk Afghanistan's descent into chaos, creating a haven for terrorists and drug dealers. It is a dangerous road which involves military casualties and enormous financial burdens. Our commitment is an exceptional one, and one that must continue until the Afghan people can assume responsibility for their own future — albeit with continuing assistance from the international community on a much smaller scale.

A Destroyed State

The principal reason the road is so hard is that as of late 2001, when the Taliban were ousted, Afghanistan was a totally destroyed state. Since the Soviet-supported Communist coup in April 1978, Afghanistan has experienced 11 years of war with the Soviets, seven years of civil war and five years of despotic Taliban rule. Its infrastructure — roads, irrigation systems, health and educational facilities, and power grids — was laid waste. Hundreds of thousands of Afghans were killed and millions fled the country, mostly to Pakistan and Iran; and the educated and technically trained migrated to the United States and Europe. In addition, many of Afghanistan's traditional structures — which previously had authority and legitimacy among the people and provided leadership, conflict resolution mechanisms, and social stability — were lost. Most important, the social fabric of the country was torn apart as families were split between those who stayed and those who fled, men died in battle, urban areas were destroyed, and dire poverty caused ethnic and religious differences to rise to the surface in the struggle for scarce resources. Commanders of forces fighting the Soviets became leaders of militias in the civil war and regional warlords in the wake of the departure of the Taliban. Almost two generations of Afghans were raised to handle Kalashnikovs instead of books and tools.

Pakistan's Role

During the years of upheaval, Pakistan's leaders saw an opportunity to exert their control over a country whose past Pushtun leadership had often called for the uniting of the two countries' Pushtuns in a new "Pushtunistan." The Pakistanis created the Taliban as an instrument of their policy. When the United States invaded

Afghanistan in late 2001 and called on Pakistan to "be for or against us," President Musharraf reversed his policy — but continued to be either unwilling or unable to crack down decisively on the radical Islamists inside Pakistan. Militants were trained, equipped, and sent into Afghanistan to fight against the "foreign infidels" who supported the new government of President Karzai. Today there exists in Afghanistan an unholy alliance between these militants, drug lords who finance and profit from the production of opium in Afghanistan, and other criminal elements.

The Past Six-and-a-Half Years

In the past six-and-a-half years there has been considerable progress toward Afghanistan's reconstruction and stabilization. An Afghan constitution was democratically ratified in early 2004, followed by presidential elections later that year and parliamentary elections in 2005. Millions of refugees have returned. More than 8,000 schools have been built; 5.7 million children, 35 percent of whom are girls, are attending them; and 140,000 teachers have been hired. Eighty-two percent of Afghans have access to basic health care today. Reconstruction of infrastructure has taken place throughout the country. Gross domestic product (GDP) has doubled since 2002, amounting today to US$21.5 billion. Military support has poured in from the U.S. and NATO to confront the insurgents who are trying to undo the progress that is being made.

But huge problems in governance, security, and development remain. The Afghan government remains unable to exert military and administrative control over large swathes of the country outside Kabul due to a number of factors: the Taliban's resurgence, with assistance from al-Qaeda and other external helpers; the inadequate strength, capacity, and effectiveness of the Afghan National

Army and Afghan National Police; and widespread and pernicious corruption in government structures, and the necessity to make deals with local and regional warlords. While macroeconomic indicators signal general progress, this may be misleading: the drug trade and development aid largely account for economic growth in a false economy. Opium production remains the mainstay of individual farmers' income in many parts of Afghanistan. Of Afghanistan's 31 million citizens, 80 percent lack electricity and only 28 percent are literate. Infant mortality has dropped but is still the second highest in the world. The rule of law has yet to be established under a poorly trained judiciary which is subject to divisive struggles over an Islamic versus a more secular legal system. The insurgency is still strong — fueled by an apparently endless supply of men from both sides of the porous, tribal border with Pakistan and supported with weapons no doubt supplied and funded in part by elements of the Pakistani army as well as by Wahhabis and other radicals in the Arab world.

Foreign Assistance

Foreign assistance to Afghanistan has been generous but nowhere near as effective as it needs to be. There are over 50,000 NATO troops, predominantly U.S., in the country; and this number continues to increase. The United States and NATO also run 25 Provincial Reconstruction Teams, which provide humanitarian and development assistance. But these forces are stretched thin in many areas; and whereas support for their deployment remains strong in the U.S., that is not the case in most other NATO countries. The approximately 55,000 Afghan troops and 75,000 police are inadequate in number and quality to provide security on their own. And as long as Pakistan does not provide full support to halt cross-border attacks, no solution to Afghanistan's security problems can be achieved.

On the developmental side, the United States has provided Afghanistan with over $23 billion in reconstruction and development assistance since 2002. In June 2008 in Paris, the international community pledged $21 billion to the development strategy presented by the Afghan government. But donors must better coordinate their assistance among themselves and with the Afghan government. To succeed, Afghan leaders and foreign donors will have to find creative compromises which will help all key elements of the fractured Afghan polity to buy into the program and process. The Afghan people too must enable government institutions to deal legitimately and credibly with security and development challenges.

Recommendations

Going forward, what should U.S. policy be? It must be a comprehensive — not piecemeal — set of actions, stressing the following five areas:

I. Security

A more secure Afghanistan not constantly threatened by insurgents is a prerequisite to success in the other four areas. To achieve this security, we must:

1. Support the Afghan government against the insurgency with our own military until such time as the Afghan security forces can do the job alone. U.S. troop levels in Afghanistan must be increased to help build the capacity of Afghanistan's own security forces and we must coordinate better strategy and tactics with them and our NATO allies.

2. Our NATO allies' involvement is vital to Afghanistan's success and we must continue to encourage their efforts. We also must continue to assure our allies that we do not intend to pass the burden onto them.

3. Reduce to the minimum civilian Afghan casualties which give rise to anti-American and anti-NATO sentiments in a country where xenophobia always lurks close to the surface. Accidental civilian deaths at the hands of allied forces play into the Taliban's favor.

4. Assist in the training and equipping of the Afghan military and police forces — which should be recruited from among local people, whenever possible, to operate in their home areas. 700 of 3,200 recently-deployed U.S. Marines are to focus specifically on building capacity for the Afghan National Army, and such efforts should clearly be further expanded.

5. Continue to urge the new Pakistani government and military to take action to prevent men and arms crossing into Afghanistan. A recent Government Accountability Office Report found that U.S. Government assistance in the Federally Administered Tribal Areas has failed, partly because of a disproportionate emphasis on military assistance to Pakistani troops over development assistance to the residents of the tribal areas. Given the current strong levels of support in Congress for such economic development programs in border regions of both countries, the incoming U.S. administration should pay much sharper and focused attention to development in the tribal areas.

II. Counter-Narcotics

Afghanistan's economy is heavily dependent on opium production and it currently yields over 90 percent of the world's opium supply. We must:

1. Focus our attention on assisting the Afghan government to develop alternative livelihoods and agricultural crops before assisting with any drastic measures to destroy opium fields. This includes supporting economic development activities, which can provide jobs and incomes that will support farmers.

2. Encourage Afghan efforts to crack down heavily on opium laboratories, storage facilities and traffickers.

3. Work with Afghan authorities to enlist farmers in opium-growing areas to develop strategies for reducing poppy growing.

III. Strengthening Governance and Improving Economic Growth

A more effective Afghan government, which can improve the lives of the Afghan people, is an essential element for a stable country. To this end we should:

1. Insist — with the new United Nations Representative in Kabul, President Karzai, and foreign donors — on tighter coordination of economic assistance, including among Provincial Reconstruction Teams, so as to maximize the effectiveness of foreign aid. At the local level, to avoid being seen as undermining the Afghan government, PRTs and other donor mechanisms must ensure that they work closely

with the government's established mechanisms for providing funds and other resource transfers.

2. Assist the Afghan government to strengthen its central and local administration so that it can absorb foreign assistance and deliver it effectively and thereby bring visible results to its people. This particularly applies to local administration, which has not been given as much emphasis as it should.

3. Under UN auspices, give technical assistance to the Afghan government for the 2009 presidential and 2010 parliamentary elections. The U.S., however, should focus not only on event-based technical assistance, but much more on helping to build sustainable electoral processes. After the 2004 and 2005 elections, considerable international support poured into Afghanistan, and then faded away once officials were elected into office. This mistake should not be repeated.

4. Support the Karzai government's efforts to strengthen the judicial system, including rooting out corruption and warlords.

5. Concentrate assistance to the higher educational sector to include programs which train Afghans needed for the country's reconstruction — especially engineers, public administrators, financial specialists, teachers, doctors and nurses, legal experts, and judicial administrators. This means an emphasis on higher and vocational education for both men and women. This work must extend beyond the nation's capital.

6. Continue to ensure that every aid project has a training component for Afghans.

7. Assist, with the help of our European and Japanese partners, the Afghan government's efforts to recruit high-quality Dari and Pashto speaking specialists from among the Afghan communities abroad who will make a long-term commitment to working in Afghanistan.

8. Help Afghanistan achieve a higher level of foreign trade and investment through its membership in the South Asian Association for Regional Cooperation and by addressing the legal obstacles and corruption which discourage the private sector.

IV. Infrastructure and Jobs

The Afghan people remain in great need of major projects to revitalize the oil and gas, power, irrigation, mining, and road-building sectors. Special attention should be given to such projects, which can create jobs and infrastructure. One example is the construction of pipelines, which would bring oil and gas from northern Afghanistan to Kabul and other population centers, fuel power plants, and fill domestic energy needs. Currently, the Asian Development Bank is funding initial work on the Turkmenistan/ Afghanistan/Pakistan/India pipeline. Positively moving toward the construction of gas and oil pipelines from Turkmenistan to Pakistan and India through Afghanistan would not only serve wider U.S. geopolitical ends by avoiding possible routes for Turkmen resources through Russia or Iran, but would also meet Afghan needs both for jobs and energy resources. In November 2007 an agreement between the Afghan government and the China Metallurgical Group to invest US$2.8 billion to develop Afghanistan's Aynak copper field in Logar Province was signed; but more can be done to explore Afghanistan's mineral wealth.

Still another need is the provision of clean water throughout the country.

V. Humanitarian Assistance

We should provide humanitarian assistance when needed in the event of such natural disasters as earthquakes and drought.

Conclusion

Afghanistan must continue to be one of the highest priorities for U.S. foreign policy. Our strategy must focus on Afghan development and security in tight coordination with the Afghan government and our international partners. It must also focus on ending the support for the Afghan insurgency from Pakistan, al-Qaeda, and other radical Islamic sources. As long as that insurgency continues, our efforts to help Afghanistan transform into a stable, secure, and prospering country will be in jeopardy.

Most critically, we must learn from our past mistakes so as to chart a more effective course.

AMERICA'S ROLE IN ASIA PARTICIPANTS

Northeast Asia Workshop Participants

CHAIR

Ambassador Han Sung-Joo
Chairman
Asan Institute for Policy Studies, Seoul

MEMBERS

CHINA
Dr. Jin Canrong
Associate Dean, School of International Studies
Renmin University of China

Dr. Wu Xinbo
Professor & Deputy Director, Center for American Studies
Associate Dean, School of International Relations and Public Affairs
Fudan University

HONG KONG
Professor James Tang
Professor, Department of Politics and Public Administration
University of Hong Kong

JAPAN
Professor Kiichi Fujiwara
Professor, Graduate School of Law and Politics
University of Tokyo

Professor Fumio Yoshino
Professor, Institute of World Studies
Takushoku University

KOREA
Professor Chun Chaesung
Associate Professor of International Relations
Seoul National University

Ms. Kang In-sun
Editorial Writer
Chosun Ilbo

MONGOLIA
Mr. Mashbat Otgonbayar
Assistant Professor, Department of Political Science
National University of Mongolia

Dr. G. Tumurchuluun
Deputy Director, Policy Planning
Monitoring and Information Division
Ministry of Foreign Affairs

RUSSIA
Dr. Andrei Lankov
Associate Professor
Kookmin University, Seoul

TAIWAN
Dr. Alexander Huang
Director, Graduate Institute of American Studies
Tamkang University

Mr. Andrew N.D. Yang
Secretary General
Chinese Council of Advanced Policy Studies

Southeast Asia Workshop Participants

CHAIR

Ambassador Tommy Koh
Chairman
Institute of Policy Studies, Singapore

MEMBERS

BRUNEI
Mr. Andrew Dy
Regional Program Manager
Asia Inc Forum

Ms. Fauziah Binte Dato Talib
Managing Partner
IQ-Quest Company

CAMBODIA
H.E. Roland Eng
Ambassador-At-Large
Ministry of Foreign Affairs

INDONESIA
Dr. Djisman Simanjuntak
Executive Director
Prasetiya Mulya Business School

Dr. Jusuf Wanandi
Vice Chairman, Board of Trustees
Center for Strategic and International Studies, Jakarta

LAOS
H.E. Vang Rattanavong
Vice Chairman
Lao National Tourism Administration

Madame Malayvieng Sakonhninhom
Acting Director General
Institute of Foreign Affairs

MALAYSIA
Dr. Zakaria Ahmad
Senior Vice President
HELP University-College

Dr. K.S. Nathan
Head, American Studies Center
National University of Malaysia

PHILIPPINES
Dr. Mely Caballero Anthony
Associate Professor
Nanyang Technological University, Singapore

Dr. Jesus Estanislao
Chairman & CEO
Institute of Corporate Directors

SINGAPORE
Mr. Manu Bhaskaran
Partner/Head, Economic Research
Centennial Group

Ambassador K. Kesavapany
Director
Institute of Southeast Asian Studies

THAILAND
Mr. Kavi Chongkittavorn
Group Editor
The Nation

Dr. Panitan Wattanayagorn
Professor of International Relations
Chulalongkorn University

TIMOR-LESTE
Mr. Jose Turquel
Chief of Staff, Office of the President
Democratic Republic of Timor-Leste

VIETNAM
Mr. Ha Kim Ngoc
Deputy Director General of the Americas Department
Ministry of Foreign Affairs

Mr. Bui Van
Deputy Editor-in-Chief
Vietnam Net

EX-OFFICIO

H.E. Dr. Surin Pitsuwan
Secretary General
Association of Southeast Asian Nations

South Asia Workshop Participants

CHAIR

Dr. C. Raja Mohan
Professor, S. Rajaratnam School of International Studies
Nanyang Technological University, Singapore

MEMBERS

AFGHANISTAN
Dr. Abduallah Abdullah
Secretary General
Massoud Foundation, Kabul;
Former Foreign Minister

Mr. Haroun M. Mir
Executive Director
Afghanistan's Centre for Policy Studies;
Director
SIG & Partners, Kabul

BANGLADESH
Professor Mustafizur Rahman
Executive Director
Centre for Policy Dialogue

Ambassador Farooq Sobhan
President
Bangladesh Enterprise Institute

INDIA
Dr. Pramit Pal Chaudhury
Foreign Editor
Hindustan Times

Ambassador G. Parthasarathy
Former Indian High Commissioner to Pakistan

NEPAL
Mr. Dipak Gyawali
Academician
Nepal Academy of Science and Technology

Dr. Bishwambher Pyakuryal
Professor of Economics
Tribhuvan University

PAKISTAN
Mr. Khalid Aziz
Chairman, Riport, and former Chief Secretary
North West Frontier Province

Ms. Nilofer Bakhtiar
Advisor to Prime Minister and Minister In-Charge
Ministry of Women's Development, with the status of Federal Minister

SRI LANKA
Mr. Mangala Moonesinghe
Director
One Text Initiative;
Former Sri Lanka High Commissioner to India

Professor Gamini Lakshman Peiris
Minister of Export Development and International Trade

American Taskforce Workshop

CHAIRS

Ambassador Michael Armacost
Shorenstein Senior Fellow, Asia Pacific Center
Stanford University

Ambassador J. Stapleton Roy
Vice Chairman
Kissinger Associates

MEMBERS

Dr. Mary Brown Bullock
Distinguished Visiting Professor of China Studies
Emory University

Mr. Ralph Cossa
President, Pacific Forum
Center for Strategic and International Studies

Ms. Catharin Dalpino
Professor of Asian Studies
Georgetown University

Dr. Elizabeth Economy
Director for Asia Studies
Council on Foreign Relations

Ambassador Theodore Eliot
Former U.S. Ambassador to Afghanistan

Dr. Ellen Frost
Visiting Fellow
Peterson Institute of International Economics

Dr. Harry Harding
Professor of International Affairs
George Washington University

Dr. Mikkal Herberg
Director, Asian Energy Security Program
National Bureau of Asian Research

Ms. Laura Hudson
Manager, International Government Affairs
Chevron Corporation

Ambassador Karl F. Inderfurth
Professor in International Affairs
George Washington University

Ms. Ellen Laipson
President and CEO
The Henry L. Stimson Center

Dr. David M. Lampton
Director of China Studies
Johns Hopkins University, SAIS

Admiral (Ret.) Michael McDevitt
Director, Center for Strategic Studies
CNA

Mr. Derek Mitchell
Senior Fellow, International Security Program
Center for Strategic and International Studies

Dr. Marcus Noland
Senior Fellow
Peterson Institute of International Economics

Mr. Bronson Percival
Senior Advisor for Southeast Asia and Terrorism in Asia
CNA

Ambassador Teresita Schaffer
Director, South Asia Program
Center for Strategic and International Studies

Mr. Scott Snyder
Senior Fellow, International Relations Program
The Asia Foundation

ABOUT THE AUTHORS

America's Role in Asia Regional Chairs:

Ambassador Han Sung-Joo
Northeast Asia Regional Chair

Professor Han Sung-Joo is Chairman of the Asan Institute for Policy Studies. He is former President, as well as Professor Emeritus at Korea University. He is also President of the Seoul Forum for International Affairs. He was the Minister of Foreign Affairs (1993-94), UN Secretary-General's Special Representative for Cyprus (1996-97), a member of the UN Inquiry Commission on the 1994 Rwanda Genocide (1999), Chairman of the East Asia Vision Group (2000-2001), and Ambassador of the Republic of Korea to the United States (2003-2005).

Professor Han taught at City University of New York (1970-78) and was a visiting Professor at Columbia University (1986-87) and Stanford University (1992, 1995). He was also a Distinguished Fellow at the Rockefeller Brothers Fund (1986-87). His English publications include *Korean Diplomacy in an Era of Globalization* (1995), *Korea in a Changing World* (1995), and *Changing Values in Asia* (1999). He has many publications in Korean, including *Nam-gwa Puk, kurigo Sekye* (The Two Koreas and the World, 2000).

Ambassador Tommy Koh
Southeast Asia Regional Chair

Tommy Koh is Ambassador-At-Large at the Ministry of Foreign Affairs, Singapore, and Chairman of the Institute of Policy Studies

304 | AMERICA'S ROLE IN ASIA

and the National Heritage Board. He was formerly Dean of the
Law Faculty at NUS. He served as Singapore's Permanent
Representative to the United Nations in New York and
Ambassador to the United States of America, Canada, and Mexico.
Ambassador Koh was also the President of the Third UN
Conference on the Law of the Sea and chaired the Earth Summit.
He was the founding Chairman of the National Arts Council and
the founding Executive Director of the Asia-Europe Foundation.
He served as the UN Secretary-General's Special Envoy to
Russia, Estonia, Latvia, and Lithuania. Ambassador Koh was also
Singapore's Chief Negotiator for the USA Singapore Free Trade
Agreement. He has chaired two dispute panels for the World
Trade Organization.

C. Raja Mohan
South Asia Regional Chair

C. Raja Mohan is currently a professor at the S. Rajaratnam School
of International Studies, Nanyang Technological University,
Singapore. Earlier, Dr. Mohan was Professor of South Asian
Studies at the Jawaharlal Nehru University in New Delhi. He also
served as the Strategic Affairs Editor of the *Indian Express* in New
Delhi, and the Diplomatic Editor and Washington Correspondent
of *The Hindu*. Dr. Mohan has a master's degree in Nuclear Physics
and a Ph.D. in international relations. He was a member of India's
National Security Advisory Board from 1998-2000 and 2004-06.
From 1992-93, Dr. Mohan was a Jennings Randolph Peace Fellow
at the U.S. Institute of Peace, Washington, D.C. His recent books
include *Crossing the Rubicon: The Shaping of India's New Foreign
Policy* (New York: Palgrave, 2004) and *Impossible Allies: Nuclear
India, United States and the Global Order* (New Delhi: India
Research Press, 2006).

America's Role in Asia American Taskforce

Chairs:

Michael H. Armacost

Michael H. Armacost is the Shorenstein Distinguished Fellow of Stanford University's Asia/Pacific Research Center, and Chairman of The Asia Foundation Board of Trustees. In his 24 years in government, he served as Undersecretary of State for Political Affairs, and U.S. Ambassador to the Philippines and to Japan. He has written or edited four books, the most recent is an analysis of American alliances in Northeast Asia.

J. Stapleton Roy

J. Stapleton Roy, a trustee of The Asia Foundation, is currently Vice Chairman of Kissinger Associates, Inc., a strategic consulting firm. He is a retired Foreign Service Officer who rose to the rank of Career Ambassador and served as the U.S. envoy to Singapore, the People's Republic of China, and Indonesia. His final posting with the State Department was as Assistant Secretary for Intelligence and Research.

Members:

Mary Brown Bullock

Mary Brown Bullock is Distinguished Visiting Professor of China Studies at Emory University, a Senior Scholar at the Woodrow Wilson International Center for Scholars, and President Emerita of Agnes Scott College. She is chair of the China Medical Board, Inc., and is a director of the Henry Luce Foundation, the Genuine Parts Company, and a trustee of The Asia Foundation.

Ralph Cossa
Ralph A. Cossa is President of the Pacific Forum CSIS in
Honolulu, a non-profit, foreign policy research institute affiliated
with the Center for Strategic and International Studies (CSIS) in
Washington, D.C. Mr. Cossa is a member of the ASEAN
Regional Forum (ARF) Experts and Eminent Persons Group. He is
a founding member and current international co-chair of the
Council for Security Cooperation in the Asia Pacific (CSCAP) and
also co-chairs the CSCAP study group aimed at halting the prolif-
eration of weapons of mass destruction in the Asia Pacific region.

Catharin Dalpino
Catharin Dalpino is Visiting Associate Professor and Director of
Thai Studies at the Edmund A. Walsh School of Foreign Service at
Georgetown University. She is a former Deputy Assistant Secretary
of State and for six years was a Fellow at the Brookings Institution.
An employee of The Asia Foundation from 1983 to 1993, she was
the Foundation's Representative for Thailand, Laos, and Cambodia
in the late 1980s.

Elizabeth Economy
Elizabeth Economy is C.V. Starr Senior Fellow and Director for
Asia Studies at the Council on Foreign Relations. She is a frequent
radio and television commentator on U.S.-China Relations, and
regularly testifies before Congress and consults for the U.S. government and corporations on Chinese environmental issues. Her most
recent book is entitled, *The River Runs Black.*

Theodore Eliot
Theodore L. Eliot Jr. served 30 years in the U.S. Foreign Service,
including as Ambassador to Afghanistan and as Executive Secretary
of the Department of State. From 1978 to 1985 he was Dean of
the Fletcher School of Law and Diplomacy at Tufts University. He

has served on numerous corporate boards, including the Raytheon Company, and non-profit boards, including The Asia Foundation, of which he has been a trustee since 1989.

Ellen Frost

Ellen L. Frost is a Visiting Fellow at the Peterson Institute for International Economics and an Adjunct Research Fellow at the National Defense University. Her prior jobs included Counselor to the U.S. Trade Representative, Deputy Assistant Secretary of Defense, Legislative Assistant in the U.S. Senate, and various positions in the private sector. Her latest book is *Asia's New Regionalism*, published in 2008.

Harry Harding

Harry Harding is University Professor of International Affairs, and former Dean of the Elliott School of International Affairs, at the George Washington University. A specialist on Asia, his major publications include, *A Fragile Relationship: the United States and China Since 1972*, and *The India-China Relationship: What the United States Needs to Know*. He is a Vice-Chairman of The Asia Foundation Board of Trustees.

Mikkal Herberg

Mikkal Herberg is Research Director of the Asian Energy Security Program at The National Bureau of Asian Research. He is also Adjunct Faculty member at the University of California, San Diego, and Adjunct Fellow at the Pacific Council on International Policy. Previously he spent 20 years in the oil industry in strategic planning roles for ARCO, where from 1997-2000 he was Director for Global Energy and Economics, responsible for worldwide energy, economic, and political analysis.

Karl F. Inderfurth

Karl F. Inderfurth is the John O. Rankin Professor of the Practice of International Affairs at George Washington University's Elliott School of International Affairs. He served as Assistant Secretary of State for South Asian Affairs (1997-2001). From 1993 to 1997 he served as the U.S. Representative for Special Political Affairs to the United Nations, with the rank of Ambassador. He is a trustee of The Asia Foundation.

Ellen Laipson

Ellen Laipson became President and CEO of the Henry L Stimson Center in 2002 after nearly 25 years of government service. Key positions included Vice Chair of the National Intelligence Council (NIC) and Special Assistant to the U.S. Permanent Representative to the United Nations. She is a trustee of The Asia Foundation.

David M. Lampton

David M. Lampton is Director of China Studies and Dean of Faculty at the Johns Hopkins School of Advanced International Studies. His most recent book, *The Three Faces of Chinese Power: Might, Money, and Minds*, was published by University of California Press in 2008. He is a trustee of The Asia Foundation.

Michael McDevitt

RADM (ret) Michael McDevitt is a Vice President at CNA, a Washington, D.C. area non-profit research and analysis company. He has been involved in U.S. security policy and strategy in the Asia-Pacific for the last 20 years, in both government policy positions and, following his retirement from the U.S. Navy, for the last decade as an analyst and commentator. He is a graduate of the University of Southern California, Georgetown University where he focused on U.S. East Asian diplomatic history, and the National War College.

Derek Mitchell

Derek J. Mitchell is Senior Fellow and Director for Asia in the International Security Program at the Center for Strategic and International Studies. Mr. Mitchell served as Special Assistant for Asian and Pacific Affairs in the Office of the Secretary of Defense from 1997-2001. He was the principal author of DoD's 1998 East Asia Strategy Report.

Marcus Noland

Marcus Noland is a Senior Fellow at the Peterson Institute for International Economics. He was a Senior Economist at the Council of Economic Advisers in the Executive Office of the President of the United States, and has held research or teaching positions at Yale University, the Johns Hopkins University, the University of Southern California, Tokyo University, Saitama University (now the National Graduate Institute for Policy Studies), the University of Ghana, the Korea Development Institute, and the East-West Center. He has served as an occasional consultant to organizations such as the World Bank and the National Intelligence Council, and has testified before the U.S. Congress on numerous occasions.

Bronson Percival

Bronson Percival, a former U.S. diplomat and professor at the U.S. Naval War College, is an expert on terrorism, Islamic radicalism, and maritime security in Asia. He divides his time between a research institution and teaching, and has recently published a book entitled, *The Dragon Looks South: China and Southeast Asia in the New Century.*

Teresita Schaffer

Teresita C. Schaffer, Director of the South Asia Program at the Center for Strategic and International Studies, was previously the

State Department's senior official responsible for South Asia. She held diplomatic posts in India, Pakistan, Bangladesh, and served as Ambassador to Sri Lanka. Her publications include, *Rising India and U.S. Policy Options in Asia,* and *Pakistan's Future and U.S. Policy Options.* She speaks 9 languages, including Urdu and Hindi. She is a trustee of The Asia Foundation.

Scott Snyder

Scott Snyder is a Senior Associate in the International Relations Program of The Asia Foundation in Washington. He joined the Foundation as Country Representative of Korea in January 2000 and moved to the Washington office in April 2004. His book, *Negotiating on the Edge: North Korean Negotiating Behavior,* was published by the United States Institute of Peace (USIP) Press in 1999.